12

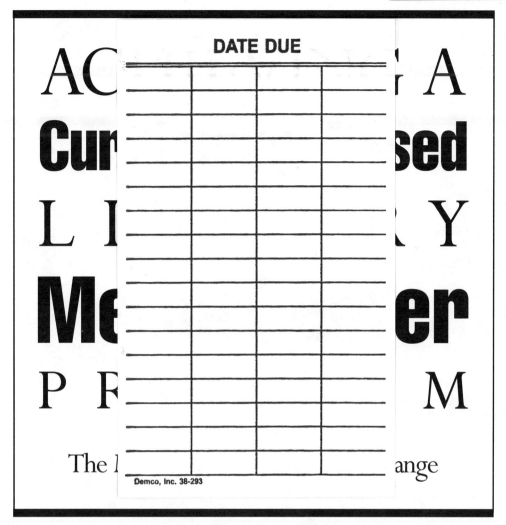

Jane Bandy Smith

American Library Association

Chicago and London

1995

Project editor: Louise Howe

Cover design: Tessing Design

Text design: Dianne M. Rooney

Composition by Publishing Services, Inc., in Perpetua using Xyvision/Linotype L330

Printed on 50-pound Glatfelter, a pH-neutral stock, and bound in 10-point C1S cover
    stock by McNaughton & Gunn, Inc.

The paper used in this publication meets the minimum requirements of American
    National Standard for Information Sciences—Permanence of Paper for Printed
    Library Materials, ANSI Z39.48-1992.∞

A substantial revision of the book *Library Media Center Programs for Middle Schools:
    A Curriculum-Based Approach,* Jane Bandy Smith (American Library Association, 1989)

Library of Congress Cataloging-in-Publication Data

Smith, Jane Bandy.
      Achieving a curriculum-based library media center program : the middle school
  model for change / by Jane Bandy Smith.
          p.   cm.
      Rev. ed. of: Library media center programs for middle schools. 1989.
      Includes index.
      ISBN 0-8389-0660-5 (alk. paper)
      1. Middle school libraries—Activity programs.   2. Library orientation for middle
  school students.   3. Media programs (Education)   I. Smith, Jane Bandy.   Library
  media center programs for middle schools.   II. Title.
      Z675.S3S653   1995
      027.8′223—dc20   95-20014

99   98   97   96   95   5   4   3   2   1

In memory of Milyn,

a most extraordinary person

The two most important functions of the middle school are human development and skill development. And these should be accepted as the responsibilities of all.

Dean John H. Lounsbury
Editor, Middle School Journal

Contents

Acknowledgments   **ix**

Preface   **xi**

1 Introducing a Curriculum-Based Program   *1*

Curriculum-Based Library Media Program Defined   *2*
Changes Required for Program Implementation   *4*
People and Change   *5*
Factors Affecting Change   *5*
Enlisting Support for Change   *6*
Overcoming Resistance to Change   *7*
Change Is Not Easier   *8*
Why Change Is Needed   *8*
A Curriculum-Based Example   *8*
Summary   *11*

2 Understanding the Needs of Students   *13*

Development of Middle Schools   *14*
Preadolescent Development   *14*
Characteristics of Middle School Programs   *14*
Organizational Elements   *16*
Student Characteristics Shape the Curriculum   *22*
Summary   *24*

3 **Gathering Information about the School** 26

A School Survey 26
The Instructional Program 32
Summary 37

4 **Planning a Curriculum-Based Program** 39

The Planning Model 39
Program Priorities 41
Library Media Committee Involvement 43
Summary 44

5 **Planning Curriculum-Based Activities** 46

Curriculum Map 46
Cooperative Planning 47
The Benefits of Collaboration 48
Instructional Design 48
Instructional Activity Plans 50
Instructional Concerns 51
Planning Aids 54
Focus on Results 57
Easing into Planning 57
Planning Record 58
Planning Frequency 59
Scheduling Library Media Activities 59
Summary 60

6 **Teaching Information Skills** 61

Information Skills Defined 61
Information Skills and Instructional Objectives 67
Relating Information Skills to Course Content 67
Summary 71

7 **Supporting Personal Development** *73*

Guidance Programs and Media Services *76*
Exploratory Programs and Media Services *80*
Community Involvement and Media Services *84*
Summary *88*

8 **Evaluating a Curriculum-Based Program** *89*

Appendixes *105*

A Program Planning Aids and Examples *105*
B Instructional Planning Aids and Examples *113*
C Record-keeping Forms *133*

Index *143*

Acknowledgments

In my life, I have been fortunate to receive help and support from a multitude of people and I am happy to have an opportunity to thank some of them.

I begin by expressing appreciation to one who encouraged me to become a library media professional. Ruth Waldrop provided a role model I have never matched. Appreciation also goes to two people who made possible and guided my early publishing efforts, William E. Hug and Kent L. Gustafson, colleagues at the University of Georgia. A number of professional leaders on the national level shared their ideas, enriching my own; these people include Shirley Aaron, Jackie Mancall, David Loertscher, Carol Kuhlthau, Carol-Ann Haycock, Frank Charles Winstead, Gordon Coleman, Phil Turner, Pamela Pritchett, Betty Morris, Martha Merrill, Marilyn Miller, Mike Eisenberg, Catherine Murphy, Retta Patrick, Aileen Helmick, Savan Wilson, Susan Bannon, Carol Kroll, and Priscilla Bennett. There are others too numerous to mention.

Thanks to the hundreds of library media professionals in Georgia and Alabama who provide such high levels of service, yet often go unrecognized. Although it was my job as a university professor and State Department of Education specialist to help them improve their knowledge and skills, they were the ones who taught me by sharing their experiences. The school library media profession is composed of remarkably talented practitioners. Although there is not enough room to name all who deserve to be named, I want to mention the following: Ann Craft Hale, Grace Burke, Paula Galland, Geraldine Bell, Margaret Blake, Teresa Culbert, Eloise Livingston, Gloria Dennard, Johnnie Sue McAnally, Mary Maude McCain, Anita Meadows, Bettye Johnson, Judy Reeves, Darnell Whited, and Paulette Williams.

A number of people helped prepare this revised edition and I owe them a debt of gratitude. Thanks to Herb Bloom, longtime editor for ALA Books, who nurtured and nudged me through the first edition and started me on the revision. To Patrick Hogan, Art Plotnik, and Louise Howe who took on the challenge when Herb decided to retire to greener pastures. Thanks to Maria Alexander whose nimble fingers do miraculous things with a computer and who helped get the ox out of the ditch and the manuscript on its way.

Let me thank the people whose love and support bring joy to each and every day—my family. To Bill David, with whom I have shared more than four decades of happy, hectic family life. To my sons David, Stuart, Bradley, and their wives, Laura, Erica, and Stephanie. Most of all, thanks to five of the world's most precious grandchildren: Ella, Will, Catherine, Stuart Elizabeth, and Foster.

Last, let me thank you the reader for your willingness to let me share my ideas, beliefs, and suggestions.

Preface

In 1988, when the first edition of this book was published, leaders in the library media field had just begun emphasizing the importance of integrating instruction in information retrieval and research skills with classroom content. Earlier attempts to do so did not convince students that library skills would help them with their studies.

Today the school library media profession is more aggressive than ever in maintaining that students must develop skill in information retrieval and use through repetition and practice as they acquire required content. Public concern and school reform pressures provide the right climate for changing old practices. Everyone recognizes that in the information age students must become more proficient in research skills. Information sources have moved dramatically from print-based to electronic, which lessens the time and skill needed for access, but increases the need to understand the intricacies of information location and retrieval. Textbooks that once offered multimedia supplements are now becoming fully integrated interactive multimedia texts. These changes propel our profession into doing things differently, and better.

This book concentrates on ways to ensure that teachers and students access the best available resources and use them in the manner that is the most effective for each individual learner. Utilization is of primary importance. Effective utilization demands strategies oriented to each student's learning style preferences and geared to performance or knowledge level. These are guidelines for curriculum-based programming.

The first edition of this book emphasized a middle school program planning model. I chose a middle school model to illustrate program planning because library media programs and middle school programs shared many common principles and problems. This edition focuses on the program design *process* rather than the model, although it continues to illustrate how a library media program can serve the specifics of a school program. More than one-third of this book is new text, and the other information retained from the older edition has been rearranged to place more emphasis on the process of program planning.

This shift is in response to teachers, library media specialists, and administrators who have described in meetings during the last five years a need for help in planning, implementing, and evaluating a collaboratively developed, curriculum-based program. Principals were concerned about making certain the library and its resources were used, and that teachers were collaborating with the library media specialist. Teachers were concerned about ensuring that every student would have access to the library and were fearful that planning would require too much time. Librarians were fearful of being rejected as peers of teachers. Few people disagree with the concept that collaboration and skill integration would increase effectiveness, but many voiced concerns over the practical problems in executing the concept. In this edition I have addressed their needs in a forthright and simple manner, including outlines or forms for practitioners implementing a curriculum-based program.

The concept that a library media program should mirror the school's program is well-founded and generally accepted. In a curriculum-based program it is emphasized and essential. Each school differs from any other, which suggests each school library media program will differ from any other. Give some thought to this idea. Even when two schools have identical grade levels, offer the same courses, and have approximately the same number of students, each school has its own character and style. The character and style are the special aspects that arise from the uniqueness of the people who populate the school. A curriculum-based library media program is built upon the framework of the school's curriculum, but it must also reflect the character and style of the school.

The services and activities in a curriculum-based program will address both the intellectual development and the personal development of students. My purpose is not to catalog the details of these services, but to help a library media specialist tailor services to the school's curriculum. As such, this book is a practical manual to adapt to the local scene.

Amidst the challenges of change, be reassured that your colleagues elsewhere are planning and implementing successful curriculum-based programs, widely heralded in their schools and communities. The goal of this book is to facilitate the process for you and your school.

Introducing a Curriculum-Based Program

Michael Fullan, a highly regarded writer and lecturer in the areas of chaos theory and educational change, writes that today's environment

> is a world where change is a journey of unknown destination, where problems are our friends, where seeking assistance is a sign of strength, where simultaneous top-down bottom-up initiatives merge, where collegiality and individualism co-exist in productive tension.[1]

A library media specialist wanting to bring about change should heed Fullan's words about simultaneous initiatives, contradictions, and tensions because change agents must keep several balls in the air at once and must be aware of the inner conflicts that occur when people try to do something in a different way.

Change usually causes some pain or at least discomfort, which is why most people avoid it. Change takes a great amount of effort and concentration, and it causes a sense of disequilibrium. So, unless people are in unsatisfying situations or can be convinced that benefits outweigh difficulties, they are unlikely to change willingly. If people are coerced to change, the change may be only superficial.

A library media specialist who wants to change from a traditional program to a curriculum-based program must expect some resistance. Although the benefits are worth the effort, persuading a school faculty to go along may be difficult and time-consuming. To be willing to change, people must be able to answer yes to the following four questions:

1

1. Will the change be personally beneficial?
2. Can I do what is required?
3. Is it worthwhile?
4. Do I trust the change agent?[2]

Some (or many) faculty members may suspect the change will benefit only the library media specialist. This is not true and experience has proven that once a faculty experiences a curriculum-based program, they understand its benefits for students and they refuse to consider going back to a traditional approach.

Curriculum-Based Library Media Program Defined

The first step in persuading a faculty to adopt a proposed change is to show them that the change will help them teach even better and will profit the students. They need to know the fundamental concepts involved in curriculum-based library media programs, and to be exposed to a working example.

The goal of a curriculum-based program is to enhance and extend classroom learning through use of varied resources and to prepare students for lifetime use of libraries and information sources. The following five principles underlie this programming approach:

1. Variety among learners is real and important,
2. Schools must recognize and meet individual needs,
3. The library media specialist is an instructional consultant,
4. Two heads are usually better than one,
5. It is appropriate for library media services to address classroom content.

In implementing these principles, the intent of a curriculum-based program is to move away from textbook-directed instruction. While textbooks may not be abandoned, they do not dominate teaching and learning as they do in traditional programs.

The framework for a curriculum-based program is, of course, the school curriculum. "Curriculum" is here interpreted as embracing everything that occurs within the school program. Approximately 85 percent of the curricular framework involves capacity building, which is the development of skills and knowledge, while the other 15 percent involves affective concerns such as development of an appreciation of self-worth, democratic values, and fair play. A curriculum-based library media program begins with the prescribed goals and objectives of the instructional program and fits resources and activities to that framework in ways that are appropriate to each learner's needs. Some students learn best through an auditory format, some need to manipulate what is to be learned, and others speed past the average learner regardless of what resources are used. Curriculum-based programming is designed to meet all these needs and more. It engages both teacher and librarian in ensuring that the delivery of curriculum material is precisely targeted to student needs. Using a variety of materials is a means not an end. The goal is to provide just the right resource and strategy so that every student is assured success in reaching every designated objective.

The purpose of a curriculum-based program is to extend and enhance what is happening in each classroom within the school. Therefore, the basic tenet of a curriculum-based program holds that it is essential for library media activities to address classroom events and instructional objectives. This idea has not been integral to traditional library media programs, which sometimes operate as islands within the schools.

The goal of a curriculum-based program is not just to incorporate multiple resources into instruction, which in some accounts appears to be the primary goal of an approach called a resource-based library media program. The terms "curriculum-based" and "resource-based" need to be compared, for they are similar in encouraging the use of multiple resources within the teaching context. Carol-Ann Haycock and David Loertscher were among the first to use "resource-based" to describe programs that incorporate resources which simultaneously teach information skills as students find and use information relevant to their studies and interests.[3] However, these two approaches to library media program planning differ because they begin from different starting points.

By definition, the curriculum shapes curriculum-based programming while resource-based programs begin with a concern about promoting library resources as learning tools. In other words, one is driven by the classroom, while the other is driven by the available resources. Both approaches are designed to develop learners' competence in finding and using information. A corollary goal of curriculum-based programs is to help teachers accomplish their instructional objectives. In effect, the library media specialist works as an instructional ally with each classroom teacher. Increased use of library resources is usually one outcome of a curriculum-based program, but it is not the rationale for implementing it. The difference between curriculum-based and resource-based programming may only be one of perspective, but to this author the differences seem important.

A curriculum-based approach begins by examining what students are supposed to know and be able to do by the end of a specific instructional time block, determining what information is involved in the content to be learned, and then aligning strategies and resources that will engage students in locating and using pertinent information as they learn what they need to know. With the shape of the library program determined by classroom events, it is essential that the media specialist have in-depth and frequent communication with every classroom teacher, as well as with special teachers such as counselors and speech therapists. Cooperative planning among professionals is a fundamental requirement of curriculum-based programs.

Planning is strengthened when two people attack the task together, because each brings special experience and information. The library media specialist is the resource specialist who knows about available information sources and how each relates to the topic being studied. The teacher is the expert with in-depth knowledge about the students, their performance, and the topic being studied.

The multitude of voices now calling for improvement of schools highlights the need for improvement in instructional effectiveness. A primary purpose of the curriculum-based program is to help teachers teach to the best of their abilities. The cry for improved student performance just might be the force that finally pushes school library media services into the center of the school program—the often stated desire of the library media profession. The key to more effective learning is having instruction suited to each student, instruction that is challenging, but not frustrating, which explains why the use of a variety of strategies and resources is important.

Although a curriculum-based program can operate within a traditional scheduling arrangement, it operates most efficiently where there is a flexible schedule for library use. A flexible schedule is one in which the media center is always available for individual and group use. Classes are not scheduled into the media center as though it were simply another classroom. Instead, groups and individuals go to the media center for a specific purpose. You might compare a media center with a flexible schedule to a Wal-Mart store. People have hundreds of reasons to go to the Wal-Mart store. The length of time each one spends there is directly correlated with his or her purpose for going. Sometimes they go only to explore what is available. When people enter, they are warmly welcomed and directed when directions are requested. The place is well stocked and a person may return an item if it is not what was wanted. A library media center should operate in similar fashion!

Changes Required for Program Implementation

A number of changes are involved in implementing a curriculum-based program. The library media specialist must know the instructional program well. Teachers must share their plans for instruction and be open to collaborative planning with the library media specialist. Administrators must be tolerant of students coming and going to the library as individuals or small groups for varying amounts of time. Media specialists must be comfortable with many different activities taking place at the same time, and they must be willing to give up control of the library media program because it will be determined in great measure by things happening in the school's classrooms.

To initiate a change from a traditional program to a curriculum-based one, a library media specialist must

- embrace the fundamental concepts,
- understand the approach well enough to articulate the benefits,
- be able to describe how it works, and then
- accept the role of change agent.

For most practitioners, the last requirement calls for gaining a new understanding of the change process in order to plan a successful campaign. It will require knowing how people react to change, analyzing how each faculty member may react, and planning ways to overcome resistance to change.

People and Change

In general, people react to change in one of three ways: they embrace it, they tolerate it, or they hate it. Gordon Coleman describes people as *innovators, middle adopters,* or *late adopters.*[4] Those easiest to persuade are the innovators. About all you have to do to persuade these people they need to change is to suggest an idea, perhaps explaining why it might be better. Look for people like this on your faculty because they can help lead the way to change.

However, most of us fall into the category of middle adopters who need to be persuaded that a proposed change has value. People like this see the status quo as an easier avenue, embracing the old saying, "if it ain't broke, don't fix it." Faculty members in this category might be convinced by a workable example that shows clear benefits, or by a conversation with a proponent from a school that has implemented the innovation. Identify these faculty members for a second phase.

Of course, the people who present the greatest challenge are the late adopters. These people fall at the far end of the change continuum and usually require some arm-twisting. Since these faculty members will be the last to try any new way of operating, do not spend an excessive amount of time trying to persuade them. Instead, wait until everyone else has converted to curriculum-based planning, and then enlist the principal's arm-twisting assistance. It may also be possible to get an early adopter to persuade them to change, particularly if the early adopter is also a dominant faculty member.

Whatever the innovation, one thing that is certain is that effecting change will require a number of strategies and result in some failures. Remember Fullan's analogy that change is a journey. A trip is never as challenge-free as the map makes it appear. Do not be dismayed by disappointments. If you expect them, they will not come as a surprise. Change agents have to tolerate temporary failures and disappointments, using them to learn better ways.

Factors Affecting Change

Everyone remembers a stirring presidential speech that rallied the country to act or an event that jelled public sentiment. Though most change is not tied to earth-shaking events or landmark speeches, there must be some driving force. What follows is a brief review of some factors that cause people to be willing to try a different approach.

Fellowship is a factor. People may go along with suggested change because they like the individual who introduces it and want to be seen as a friend. Or, the person suggesting the change may have position or power that others want to connect with. Some people are particularly persuasive and the force of their personality encourages change. This factor indicates how important it is that the library media specialist have a good relationship with members of the faculty. A study several years ago suggested the impact a library media specialist's personality has on program success. The personality factor can also be important in persuading others to try something new.[5]

Change can also be mandated by authorities. However, when change is mandated routine monitoring is necessary because those who must implement the change have not bought into it. They may appear to, but good will is rarely sustained. A change may be undertaken because of a problem or condition that creates so much dissatisfaction or disharmony that it must be solved and the only viable solution calls for change. One unfortunate example is when police must patrol high school halls.

The two change strategies used most often by a library media specialist seeking support from teachers and administrators are fellowship and education. One appeals to the soul and the other to the mind. The fellowship strategy is based on the assumption that good interpersonal relations secure support. Susan Curzon reminds those who would be change agents about how important it is to show respect for others, to be open to others, to be credible, and to keep communication channels open.[6] A library media specialist who shuns involvement in schoolwide activities or one who prefers to be an isolated professional in the library media center is unlikely to be a successful change agent.

Enlisting Support for Change

The fellowship factor may rest upon the relationships between the library media specialist and the teachers. At a minimum, these are important relationships. However, an influential advocate—the principal or popular teacher—can be very helpful in persuading others to try the new approach. Once you identify supportive staff members, be certain they have the information they need about curriculum-based programming. This is where the education factor comes into play. The easiest way to explain how the new system works is to arrange a joint visit to a school where a curriculum-based or resource-based program has been implemented. People at the site can explain how it works and the benefits. The library media specialist at your state education department should be able to suggest visitation sites. If you can't find a site to visit, it may be possible to borrow a videotape showing such a program. Pris Seeley, library media specialist at Farley Elementary School in Huntsville, Alabama, made a videotape about her school's curriculum-based program that she shares with other faculties. The Georgia Department of Education has several videotapes that illustrate a curriculum-based approach, although the intent of those tapes is to explain flexible scheduling.[7]

If there is not a visitation site nearby, you can illustrate how a curriculum-based program works by planning a few curriculum-based activities within the traditional library program. If possible, get a teacher to plan the library media activities with you so that they are appropriately tied to real instructional objectives and actual student needs. If you cannot find someone to work with you, plan the activities on your own and arrange for teachers to visit the library media center to observe them.

It is important to gain the principal's understanding and support. Although all principals want successful school programs, they may not see the library program as integral to school success. Unfortunately too many principals see the library as only an added feature of the school, a place where pleasant but not critical things take place. If this is the situation in your school, simply maintaining that a curriculum-based program will help fuel successful learning will not be enough to convince most administrators that it is time to change. The principal will need to understand exactly what happens in a curriculum-based program, how it differs from the approach currently used, and what difference it can make in student achievement.

Even when principals see merit in curriculum-based programming and support the change, competing demands often pressure them to stay with the status quo. For example, a principal is caught in the middle when teachers want the library to operate as it always has and do not want to spend time planning and sharing evaluative data with the library media specialist. The library media specialist lobbies against this practice because it limits access and shortchanges the students. In such a contest, sheer numbers favor the teachers' point of view. If change is to take place, the media specialist will need to present enough evidence to persuade both principal and teachers to join the movement.

Overcoming Resistance to Change

Persuading teachers to collaborate in planning curriculum-based library media activities can be even more difficult than convincing an administrator that it is a desirable change. There are more people to convince and the change may add to the teachers' responsibilities. Many teachers are not experienced in joint planning and most teachers feel overburdened. A library media specialist seeking to bring about change needs to anticipate and understand the possible obstacles.

Teachers may resist the move to curriculum-based or resource-based programs because these programs are often bundled with flexible scheduling. Teachers in elementary and middle schools who are accustomed to dropping the class off at the library and heading for a free period may resist change because of the flexible scheduling component. They resent the loss of precious class-free time. In high schools, where flexible schedules are common, teachers resist the extra duty of planning with another person, whether it is a teacher or librarian.

Perhaps the best way to persuade teachers to change to curriculum-based programming is to illustrate how it can help them achieve their teaching objectives and how it enhances student learning. This is possible because the objectives of the library media program will match the classroom teachers' objectives. The variety of approaches that are possible when classroom activities are connected with library media center activities will help teachers better meet the individual needs and interests of students.

Teachers are aware of the many ways in which students differ, and most teachers are frustrated because they are unable to address those differences adequately. Showing how curriculum-based programming can help address individual needs can be a giant step toward getting a teacher's participation.

Change Is Not Easier

A curriculum-based program is more demanding to plan and deliver than a traditional library media program. It requires the library media specialist to have knowledge and skills beyond providing information, telling stories, booktalking, and teaching library skills. In order to undertake a curriculum-based program, a library media specialist must know and stay abreast of general educational principles. This means

- having in-depth information about the specific school,
- knowing the characteristics of the school level,
- being familiar with characteristics of all the students,
- being informed about the total instructional program,
- knowing how to plan and evaluate instruction, and
- being skillful in planning collaboratively.

These requirements add the dimensions of program designer, teacher, and facilitator to those of the traditional librarian. The role emphasizes the educator aspect of school librarianship and underscores the importance of working with and for teachers as well as students.

Why Change Is Needed

A major problem in schools today is that many teachers still teach the same way they were taught. In a highly regarded and much publicized study, John Goodlad and his associates looked at classrooms across the United States and found that, on the whole, teachers at all levels apparently did not know how to vary their instructional procedures, did not want to, or had some kind of difficulty doing so.[8] In the face of public cries for a higher level of student performance, teachers who do not know how to vary instruction need an ally. That ally can be a properly trained and motivated library media specialist who offers a curriculum-based program. This is not just theory. It is happening; it is working in schools of every type and level. This book provides a step-by-step plan for such a program and applies the process using a middle school model.

Once teachers understand the purpose and principles of a curriculum-based program, they need to see one in action. If a visit to an existing program cannot be arranged, it will be necessary to plan and prepare an example to take place at your own school. Letting teachers see the concept in action can plant the seed for change. When the teachers see the students' interest and enthusiasm about finding information that is interesting and useful in their class work, that seed may germinate.

Showing how the program can work may mean you have to plan, prepare, and provide a range of class-related activities on your own. However, it is often possible to enlist the aid of an early-adopter colleague.

A Curriculum-Based Example

Figure 1.1 illustrates how a curriculum-based program for a fifth-grade class studying the Colonial Period in United States history might unfold. The sample program would take place during a scheduled library period. While

FIGURE 1.1 *A curriculum-based example*

Social Studies Instructional Objective

Analyze the emergence of the American culture during colonization.

Activity Plan

Group	# of Students	Activities and Time Required
Group 1	4 students	Research clothing worn in the colonial period and illustrate typical dress. *Evaluation:* Analyze differences and explain why those differences are found. *2 periods required*
Group 2	6 students	Select music of the time period to demonstrate a dance popular during the time period. *Evaluation:* From ten recorded selections, select the two that demonstrate music popular during the colonial period. *2 periods required*
Group 3	3 students	Calculate buggy travel time to specific places and develop a travel guide of sites to see. *Evaluation:* Calculate problems related to travel at given rates of speed and distances. *2 periods required*
Group 4	10 students	Locate Colonial Williamsburg on a map, watch the video, *Colonial Williamsburg,* then discuss similarities and differences with today regarding food, schooling, homes, daily activities, etc. *Evaluation:* Select the most significant difference and write a paper defending the selection. *1 period required*

Individual Activities

Identify trades practiced in colonial time and draw pictures of the tools that were used.

Select one trade practiced in the colonies to learn about in depth and explain it to others through writing, drawing, or making a video.

Identify an artist of the day and locate pictures by him or her. Explain your choice.

Identify a poet or writer of the day and locate at least one work. Explain your choice through the format of an audiotape.

this example targets an elementary school or middle school grade, the same approach works when a high school grade or subject is addressed. Planning begins with the classroom instructional objectives, activities are generated to teach or extend those objectives, a strategy is devised to engage students in groups or as individuals, and a method of evaluating the activity is determined.

Our example uses four small groups of students, perhaps grouped according to interest. Each group participates in one activity. Individual activities are available for any group finishing ahead of schedule or for group members who want to move to a different activity. Students can rotate from group to group, or groups can rotate from activity to activity. Adaptability is paramount, which suggests why flexible scheduling is better for a curriculum-based program than set schedules where students must come and go according to bells and the clock. Although this example was developed to show how a curriculum-based program could be illustrated within a traditional library schedule, when a real program is in place, student groups from several grades pursuing numerous instructional objectives would be in the library at the same time.

Because the library media activities and objectives are consistent with the classroom objectives, they can take place in either the classroom or the library. Evaluation can occur in either place. Directions for an activity can be provided by either the teacher or the library media specialist, but it is critical that both professionals know what is taking place and when. In curriculum-based programming, the teacher and library media specialist work as a team in making decisions, and each one bears equal responsibility for student progress. The library media specialist makes suggestions regarding the activities, but the teacher has final responsibility for grouping students, assigning students to certain activities, setting time limits, and identifying the desired products.

Capture the interest of teachers by showing them what takes place in the media center when a curriculum-based program is implemented. Remind them that the objectives are the same as those being addressed in the classroom. Explain how much their involvement would add to program planning. Their experience and in-depth knowledge of each student's achievement level and interests would make planning more precise.

Once a teacher expresses interest in the program, ask him or her to stay in the media center to interact with the students as they engage in the activities you have planned. Teachers who stay are likely to begin suggesting alternative activities or resources. Back in the classroom, they will remind students how the library information relates to classroom content. When that happens, you have the teacher hooked! Little by little, this approach will demonstrate the value of integrating library media use with classroom content.

Regardless of whom you are trying to educate about the merits of curriculum-based programming, focus on the question: What is the most advantageous practice for our students? Most principals and teachers do not understand either the process or the advantages of curriculum-based programming because they have never experienced it. However, most of them want whatever will benefit the students. So remember that student benefit is the prime selling point for curriculum-based programming. This approach assists teachers in doing their best for the learners, but the focus is on student learning.

Despite your best efforts, it may be necessary to compromise in the beginning on an interim approach that combines both traditional library service and curriculum-based programming. However, be confident that total change is inevitable because schools that have implemented these programs have found them warmly embraced by administrators, teachers, parents, and students. Perhaps knowing this will help you keep your eye on the eventual goal of having full-time curriculum-based service. The following chapters employ a middle school model to elaborate curriculum-based services.

Summary

Initiating a curriculum-based program usually requires change and change is rarely easy. However, the results are worth the effort. Once a library media specialist is committed to curriculum-based programming, she or he should plan a campaign for change. Remember that people are more likely to accept change when the change agent is open, is accepting, and communicates clearly.

The first step is to inform other faculty about the elements of curriculum-based programming. Then, illustrate how a curriculum-based program operates. This may be the most effective way to enlist others in supporting a change from traditional to curriculum-based services. Keep the focus on benefits to students. These benefits accrue from the relevance to classroom instruction and the opportunities to meet individual needs. While traditional programs may be enjoyable and help students learn, aligning library activities with specified school objectives enhances the value of library media services.

Notes

1. Michael Fullan, *Change Forces: Probing the Depths of Educational Reform* (London: Falmer, 1993), vii–viii. In this book, Fullan shares eight basic lessons about the new paradigm of change. One lesson reminds us that problems are inevitable and important in helping us learn. Fullan cautions change agents to expect an implementation gap when initiating a new approach. Even with successful changes, there is a period when things appear not to be working as planned.

2. Clay Carr and Mary Fletcher, *The Manager's Troubleshooter: Pinpointing the Causes and Cures of 125 Tough Supervisory Problems* (Englewood Cliffs, N.J.: Prentice Hall, 1990), 22.

3. See works such as Carol-Ann Haycock's "Resource-Based Learning: A Shift in the Roles of Teacher, Learner," *NASSP Bulletin* 75 (1991): 15–22; and David L. Loertscher's *Taxonomies of the School Library Media Program* (Englewood, Colo.: Libraries Unlimited, 1989).

4. J. Gordon Coleman, Jr., "Managing Change," in *Renewal at the Schoolhouse*, ed. Ben B. Carson and Jane Bandy Smith (Littleton, Colo.: Libraries Unlimited, 1993), 75–84.

5. Barbara Herrin, Louis R. Pointon, and Sara Russell, "Personality and Communications Behaviors of Model School Library Media Specialists," *Drexel Library Quarterly* 21 (Spring 1985): 69–90.

6. Susan C. Curzon, *Managing Change: A How-to-Do-It Manual for Planning, Implementing, and Evaluating Change in Libraries* (New York: Neal-Schuman, 1989).

7. Priscilla A. Seeley has presented her programming ideas at several national and state conferences, including the American Association of School Librarians' Sixth National Professional Conference in Baltimore, Maryland. Mrs. Seeley is on staff at Farley Elementary School, 2900 Green Cove Road, S.W., Huntsville, Alabama 35803, and can be reached by phone at 205-532-3009. The Georgia Department of Education is located at 2054 Twin Towers East, Atlanta, Georgia 30305; phone 404-656-2418.

8. John I. Goodlad, *A Place Called School* (New York: McGraw-Hill, 1984), 105–6.

2

Understanding
the Needs
of Students

The library media specialist must thoroughly understand the school environment before trying to implement change. The purpose of this chapter and the next is to cover information a middle school media specialist would need to know; therefore, information specific to that age group is provided. No matter what the grade level, school media specialists should be sensitive to the developmental stages of the student.

To tailor a library media program to fit a school's program, the media specialist must first understand the school level characteristics. In a middle school, for example, the media specialist should be able to answer questions such as the following and to know how the answers reveal middle level education philosophy:

- What are the major concepts of middle school education?
- What instructional methods are preferred?
- How are activities scheduled?
- How are students grouped?
- What provisions are found in appropriate facilities?

The answers to these questions impact a curriculum-based library media program because the program must mirror the school program. This is also true for a media program at an elementary or high school.

Development of Middle Schools

Dr. William Alexander, a University of Florida education professor, is credited as the "father of the middle school movement." He was the first person to call for a new way of educating preadolescents as educators learned more about the development of youngsters between the ages of ten and fourteen. To him, existing school practices seemed inappropriate. Alexander, in a 1960 conference speech to junior high educators, endorsed development of a school program that was based on student needs instead of traditional practices.[1]

Many other educators agreed that junior high programs did not serve the needs of preadolescent students adequately because those programs were subject-dominated, stressed conformity, limited peer interaction, offered few electives, encouraged competition, and fostered premature sophistication. For the most part, junior high programs replicated senior high practices—shuttling students in groups from course to course like a factory assembly line. Most high school programs fit students into the program's parameters rather than altering the program to suit the students' needs. Alexander proposed a school program that would reverse that situation, responding to the great variations within and between preadolescent students. Educators who rallied to Alexander's call for change continued to explore ways to provide a school program with a stable but flexible framework that would allow each preadolescent student to develop as an individual yet feel part of a group.

Preadolescent Development

Preadolescents are in a complex period of life that is greatly affected by the chemical changes within their bodies that signal the onset of puberty. Professionals who work with preadolescents caution that the maturation process is very complex because although students go through similar changes, change occurs for each student at a different rate and in a unique pattern. Because of the multitude of changes, Donald Eichhorn originated the term "transescents." to describe youngsters between the ages of ten and fourteen. Eichhorn felt the word described these youths as crossing over from childhood to adolescence.[2]

Characteristics of Middle School Programs

Providing a school program that is personalized enough to meet the needs of constantly changing individuals demands real effort from the faculty. They must be skillful both in teaching and in human relations. They must be dedicated to responding to the needs of young adolescents, for it is those needs that define the school program. To better understand the complex demands placed on middle school educators read the statement of school purpose written by students, teachers, and parents at Harper's Choice Middle School in Columbia, Maryland. It gives testament to what the school community believes to be essential.

> As Middle School Students We Believe That . . .
>
> We need to develop our independence through controlled guidance by teachers. Socializing as well as learning must be incorporated into the program.

We are too mature for elementary school but not ready for high school. We should be provided with an opportunity to grow and yet still act our age. We need a different freedom in a situation where boundaries are clear and are enforced without any favoritism or prejudice.

We are uniquely different. We need to learn interesting and useful subjects from caring, well-prepared teachers who accept us and help us enjoy learning in an active educational program.

We must be given opportunities and guidance in working with our peers. We need to learn to judge our own progress both as individuals and as groups.

We should have a program which enables us to mature at our own rate and still be part of the crowd. We need to learn the things necessary for higher education and for adult life, while gaining and maintaining friendships. We especially need variety and challenge.

Their statements stress the importance of both skill development and human development, which Dean Lounsbury cited in the epigraph at the beginning of this book. It is a call for a program that provides controlled guidance, clear boundaries, fairness, acceptance, interaction among peers, self-examination, self-paced instruction, variety, and challenge. Consider the content of their statements in combination with eighteen program criteria for a "true" middle school shown below.[3]

1. Continuous progress program
2. Multi-material approach
3. Flexible schedules
4. Appropriate social experiences for early adolescents
5. Appropriate physical activities
6. Intramural activities
7. Team teaching
8. Planned gradualism from childhood to adult independence
9. Exploratory-enrichment studies
10. Guidance services
11. Independent study
12. Basic skill remediation or enhancement
13. Creative experiences
14. Provision for student need of a security group
15. Individualized and nonthreatening evaluation
16. Community relations and involvement

17. Stress on student services

18. Auxiliary staffing

A middle school program is a paradox. The program must offer abundant variety in instructors, materials, topics, experiences, etc., yet there must be stability and sustained guidance. Rules must be clearly established and firmly enforced, but with enough flexibility to consider the circumstances; students must participate in making rules and their opinions must be taken seriously. Middle school programs must provide frequent opportunities for peer interaction, but also ensure times for quiet introspection and reflection. Students in middle schools love to be busy, but the faculty must be certain that students do not become overexerted. Preadolescents want to be seen as adults, but it is important that their activities be appropriate for their age. They act like an adult one minute and like a toddler the next. Adults who work with them must ensure that they are not pushed too quickly into competitive encounters or social maturity.

Organizational Elements

A library media specialist preparing to implement a curriculum-based program will need to understand how and why the school operates as it does. This means understanding the instructional methods being used, the way students are grouped for activities, and how classes and events are scheduled (across the school and within each teaching unit).

Instructional Methods

Because middle grade students are as diverse in the rate and level of their basic skills achievement as they are in everything else, they need varied instruction. Some youngsters still need primary drill and practice, while others need to apply already developed skills in analyzing and solving increasingly complex problems. Skill development—developing or extending basic skills in reading, language, and math—is a key goal in any middle school program. The entire school faculty must be concerned that every student achieves competence in the basic skill areas because these skills provide the foundation for independent study and learning. School personnel must ensure that each student continues to progress in the areas of skill development.

A school program that reflects middle school principles will have a clear mission with established goals and objectives. However, the instructional strategies and activities used to reach those goals will vary according to each student's needs. Although this approach is often called *individualized* instruction, it is really *personalized* instruction because student needs usually fall into patterns that permit small groups to be addressed similarly and simultaneously. Whatever the name, individualized or personalized instruction is always demanding to plan and to prepare. In the middle school setting the task of meeting individual needs is even more complex than at other school levels because of the constantly changing nature of the students.

Middle school students change almost from moment to moment. One minute a sixth grade student may act like a six-year-old, and the next minute like a twenty-year-old. There is a steady move toward maturity but getting there involves many stalls, starts, and spurts. Students are maturing physically, broadening socially, and becoming increasingly capable of learning more complex and abstract concepts, but in instruction most of them still need concrete examples, hands-on experience, and a guiding hand. During the middle school years, most students make the transition from childhood dependence on adults to independence and self-reliance. They move from self-concern to family-concern and on to broader community-concern. However, they do nothing at a predictable pace. Their development is a complex phenomenon that seems to surprise even themselves.

An instructional program in which teachers try to adapt to each student's constantly changing needs, while at the same time reaching established objectives, is a program that demands flexibility within structure. A middle school teacher needs an instructional plan that provides many paths to the same objective. Each path is laid by a different type of instructional resource, or a different delivery mode, or a different strategy to engage the student. Each path must help at least one student move from level to level in a developmental learning journey, ultimately reaching a common objective. This does not suggest that every child will learn the same amount or the same things, but that all students in the class will reach a level of understanding about each instructional objective. Making certain each student stays on the path requires monitoring progress constantly and making adjustments as needed. These requirements mean that planning between the teacher and the library media specialist must be ongoing.

Middle school students need to be actively involved in their learning. This idea is being increasingly emphasized as research continues to show that inquiry, cooperative techniques, and hands-on activities are effective instructional strategies. When students must figure out the answers after being given the tools and necessary background information, more learning takes place than when teachers spout information from their own fountain of knowledge and expect students to soak it up and then spit it out. John Dewey, many years ago, shared an example of how inquiry, hands-on, and cooperative activities stimulated learning.

> [T]he children are first given the raw material—the flax, the cotton plant, the wool as it comes from the back of the sheep (if we could take them to the place where the sheep are sheared, so much the better). Then a study is made of these materials from the standpoint of their adaptation to the uses to which they may be put. For instance, a comparison of the cotton fiber with wool fiber is made. I did not know, until the children told me, that the reason for the late development of the cotton industry as compared with the woolen is that the cotton fiber is so very difficult to free by hand from the seeds. The children in one group worked thirty minutes freeing cotton fibers from the boll and seeds, and succeeded in getting out less than one ounce. They could easily believe that one person could gin only one

pound a day by hand, and could understand why their ancestors wore woolen instead of cotton clothing.[4]

In this example, students take responsibility for their own learning and then share what they have learned with the others. Think how much more likely it was that those students would value the technology of the cotton gin than if they had been told of its value in a lecture, or had seen other children explain the value in a television program.

The teacher's role in instruction is to engage the students in inquiry. Skillful teaching is managing the situation so that students learn through finding their own answers to questions. This must be achieved through structured experimentation and investigation. This approach to learning is especially important for middle school students because many of them are still at the concrete stage where they need to see, handle, measure, count, and examine in order to learn. Many students in the ten-to-fourteen age bracket are not yet mature enough to manipulate abstractions mentally, nor to generalize, nor to make inferences.[5] The groundwork needed for higher-order thinking is gained through concrete experiences and development of basic skills. Because students vary in their place on the continuum as they move from concrete to abstract learning and in their degree of skill development, a broad range and variety of learning experiences must be ensured.

Effective instruction requires the availability of abundant supplementary materials on all topics in the school program. The need for a variety of materials is readily apparent when anyone visits a middle school class. Students will be reading on at least six or seven different levels of difficulty, there will be tactile learners who learn best through a hands-on method and others who like to watch and listen, and there will be students with either slight or significant handicaps. The students in any given room will have interests that range from motorcycles to butterflies, and each student will have had different experiences before coming to class. For the instructional program to be tailored to fit each student, it is obvious that many variations are needed. A teacher cannot provide the necessary variations with one textbook or by moving students in lock-step fashion through a set schedule. This need for a variety of materials is one reason why the library media center is an essential element in a middle school—not a frill or an added feature!

Some middle schools use a continuous progress program that requires teachers to measure individual skill achievement on a frequent and routine basis. This type of skill development course is partitioned into discrete steps, allowing each student to move from one level to the next as she or he is ready. Each student's beginning level is determined by a test of prior learning. As a student then moves from step to step, the pace should stimulate but not frustrate him or her. The teacher must monitor performance regularly and closely, allowing the student to set the pace as long as there is forward movement. Yet if the student falters, the teacher must be alert to introduce a new element into instruction, or to remove a learning block, or to challenge with a new direction. This method allows instruction to be individually tailored, although not necessarily individually delivered.

Middle school teachers need to be comfortable with change because teaching strategies and materials must frequently be altered to meet changing student needs. Students move through material at different speeds, they have different interests, and they are motivated differently, which means that materials must be routinely adjusted within each student's range and experience. An item that was just right for a student yesterday may be all wrong tomorrow. Diversity is a keyword in preadolescent instruction. Not only do learners differ in their preferred learning mode, they function at various stages of development and have different interests. These variations present complexities that require wide variation in content, degree of sophistication, and reading level.

Student Grouping

Middle grade students need to work with a wide variety of both students and adults. They need to experience varied working arrangements—individually, in small groups, and in large groups. Because of the frequent need to change group size and membership, an open school with movable walls is a popular arrangement for a middle school facility. This arrangement allows for easy movement of students from one group to another.

Another popular arrangement is to section the school into "pods," each housing a grade level or team of teachers. A pod arrangement provides a feeling of a home within the school, which responds to the students' need for security. This arrangement also eliminates the necessity of changing rooms for different courses, those hall-crowding experiences that often lead to a need for disciplinary action. Movement or changing activities in a middle school program is dictated by the program's needs rather than by a bell sounding in the hall in response to the clock.

Because of the constant grouping and regrouping that occurs in a middle school program, it is best to have buildings that permit various sized groups simultaneously involved in a range of activities. Such features as open, multi-use areas with walls that can be moved and furnishings that can be easily rearranged are ideal. Carpeted floors allow student groups to sit on the floor, and also muffle sound caused by frequent moving about.

While it is important for preadolescents to find suitable adult behavior patterns, it is perhaps even more important for them to feel accepted by their peers. Kids their own age usually provide a nonthreatening opportunity to see how people will react to what they say and do. Interaction gives them opportunities that are similar to holding up a mirror. They not only see how others react, but they find out how it feels to act in certain ways. We hope they will select appropriate behaviors to carry into their adult lives.

Concerns of preadolescents about how others perceive them and about how they fit in the group should never be minimized by adults who work with them. Middle school program planners make certain that all students are given numerous opportunities to role-play, discuss, and dramatize human interaction situations. These opportunities allow them to explore their insecurities without having to reveal their own problems and fears.

Group activities are important for ten- to fourteen-year-olds, but they also need time alone. Recognizing these needs, middle school programs are planned to provide students time and places for individual activities and introspection. The media center is a perfect place for quiet corners that are tucked away for reading, viewing, studying, or just thinking. Conversely, it can also be a creative center where students gather to work on group projects.

Home Base

Every preadolescent needs the security provided by having at least one adult in the school who is fully informed about his or her background, characteristics, past performance, and previous experiences—someone who shows particular concern about him or her, and who provides a parent-like association. For this reason, most middle schools use some type of a "home-base" or advisor/advisee scenario where a student develops an in-depth relationship with at least one teacher. In today's society with the proliferation of single-parent homes, teenage suicide, drug culture, and frequent mobility, this aspect of the middle school program is especially important.

The conflicting needs of preadolescent students are evident when one compares their need for the security of a home-base teacher with their equal need to interact with a wide variety of adults. Being able to associate with a variety of adults lets a youth test how to relate to others. Preadolescents are constantly trying out behaviors to test the reactions of others. Awareness of this practice can help adults who might be tempted to judge their actions as enigmatic and erratic remember it is only a phase of maturation. It is their trial-and-error way of determining how they should act when adult.

Students need to be exposed to good role models because of their propensity for copying others. Middle school teachers realize they are role models, and they are particularly concerned with setting a good example. They strive to be human as well as humane.

Schedules

Just as flexible facilities accommodate a middle school program, flexible or block schedules accommodate the instructional program. A flexible schedule is typical for middle schools because it makes it easier for teaching teams to develop interdisciplinary courses, since they can plan activities for blocks of time rather than forty-five minute periods. This approach provides a more leisurely approach to learning because time periods are controlled by the teaching team instead of the clock. The benefits are evident—it means the group discussion can continue instead of being terminated just because the clock strikes the hour, or a practice session can continue once a skill has been mastered. In the past, too much learning was lost because the bell rang and it was necessary to stop—ready or not!

These frustrations are reduced in most middle schools because a schedule with lengthy time blocks gives instructors the flexibility to adjust their schedule without having to reschedule the entire school. For example, if the teaching team decides more time is needed for the next three days on geography, they are able to shift time from another subject. Time can be shifted the other way in days to come.

Block scheduling also benefits the library media program because it provides scheduled opportunities for teachers and the media specialist to meet for planning and evaluating. For example, if a school used a schedule similar to that shown in Figure 2.1, a media specialist could meet with each teaching team while students participated in art, music, or physical education. Or the media specialist could meet with each team on a different day of the week. Planning is more likely to bear results when time is regularly set aside during the school day than when it must be done either before or after school hours.

FIGURE 2.1 *Block schedule used at Harper's Choice Middle School*

	Sixth Grade		Seventh Grade		Eighth Grade	
8:30						
9:00	Home Base		Art Music P.E.		Basics	
9:30			Exploratory	Planning		
10:00						
10:30	Basics				Art Music P.E.	
11:00			Basics		Exploratory	Planning
11:30						
12:00	Lunch					
12:30	Art Music P.E.	Planning	Lunch			
1:00	Exploratory		Home Base		Lunch	
1:30						
2:00	Basics		Basics		Basics	
2:30						
3:00					Home Base	

Student Characteristics Shape the Curriculum

The developmental changes in preadolescents are both exciting and unnerving, and they do create conflicts within the student and with the student's environment. Therefore, middle school program planning must provide ways to manage and respond to these expected changes.

Programs that have firm, but not rigid, structures work best. Students this age are reassured by established boundaries and stated expectations, despite their frequent wails against them. Boundaries and clear expectations provide students with security and stability. Certainly the students are expected to push against those boundaries, but this pushing is a growth exercise that helps each child define him- or herself and helps shape an understanding of how the world operates. Their struggles, however, need to occur in a supportive environment because of the many uncertainties that fill their world. The following sections highlight some of the many changes and conflicts that permeate the lives of middle school students and illustrate ways in which middle school programs can respond.

Changing Bodies, Health, and Physical Education

Sudden growth spurts cause preadolescents to appear awkward or clumsy. Some students seem to grow overnight and body parts are not always proportionate. Rapid growth can result in clumsiness, and it is not unusual to see preadolescents bumping into things or stumbling. When this happens a student feels self-conscious and embarrassed.

Regular exercise and planned physical movement help middle school students gain poise and muscular control, so physical education becomes an important facet in a middle school program. It is not just play. This is one reason gyms are important features in a middle school plant. The physical education program contributes meaningfully to both a student's physical and self-concept development.

Cooperative games rather than competitive events are the focus of the sports program in a middle school. Youths who are already insecure do not need the dismay of a poorly kicked ball that results in a losing effort for the school. This is why athletic events in middle school programs usually are planned as intramural activities—it is better for preadolescents to be involved in sports that provide learning situations than to be competing for positions or points. They need to develop their own athletic capabilities as their bodies mature, and to experience the belonging of team participation.

Body changes greatly inhibit youngsters between the ages of ten and fourteen. One boy will be the size of an average adult while the next one is more than a foot shorter. One girl will have developed breasts while the next has not. Body changes make preadolescents uncomfortable. If a student's body is not changing, he or she is fearful that something is wrong. If it is changing, he or she is embarrassed. These students need to be reassured that although individuals undergo body changes in different patterns and develop to different degrees, everyone's experiences are similar. Middle school programs provide courses in health and human development to help these students better understand that body changes are a natural development. These courses foster self-concept and help establish positive sex roles.

Changing Self-Concepts and Guidance

Although physical change may be the most evident, it is often emotional and social development that causes the most problems for preadolescents. The constant change invading their lives causes feelings of disequilibrium— uncertain feelings that are revealed by the way they react to a situation or exhibit conflicting actions. Often the actions of preadolescents frustrate adults because these youngsters seem to be totally different from one day to the next, or even one hour to the next. Youngsters caught in the grip of change need frequent contact with patient adults who can help them understand who they are. Counselors expect students to try out behaviors in their search for appropriate actions. We are reminded by Joan Lipsitz, former director of the Center for Early Adolescence that

> Adolescents depend upon others to reflect to them a positive, realistic image of self that can be integrated with a personal inner image. They are dependent upon society to have a coherent sense of purpose for its young people with which, and in opposition to which, they can define themselves.[6]

Most preadolescents tend to be unrealistic and egotistical in their inner view of themselves. They are overly concerned with themselves and how others react to them. Often they believe that everyone else is watching and concerned with them, and frequently these feelings cause them to act out. This behavior makes them appear silly and seems exaggerated to people who fail to put their actions into the perspective of their age.

Preadolescents often feel they are impervious to death. Unfortunately this misplaced belief may result in their taking foolish actions—sometimes even life-threatening actions. In order to develop healthy self-concepts these students need to be reminded frequently that they are important, unique individuals; but it is equally important for them to have a realistic view that they are not always the center attraction. They need a real-world view of the dangers inherent in risk-taking actions, realizing that foolish actions can result in injury or death. The simultaneous need to be reassured of their importance and reminded they are not always the central concern illustrates how much of a balancing act this age requires from adults who work or live with them.

Peer pressure is such a strong influence in preadolescent years that it often creates family friction. Students this age are overly concerned with the opinions of others. Youngsters may appear to be indifferent, but if they believe other people see them as unworthy or as failures, they often will view themselves in that way. Or even worse, they will live up to a poor image! Middle school faculties realize that it is important for every student to have success, for it is only on the basis of successful experiences that students can engage in healthy self-analysis or come to understand that a person can learn from positive criticism.

For adults who work with them the most frustrating elements of pre-adolescent emotional development are the dramatic mood changes and the tendency to overreact to situations. Extreme reactions may occur because a youngster feels inadequate or uncertain, but it can also be because he or she is physically tired. Middle school programs incorporate features that help students maintain emotional equilibrium, such as well-staffed guidance programs and "home-base" teachers who provide a constant adult ally.

Changing Judgment and Student Government

Middle school students have a conflicting approach to justice. On one hand they are quick and harsh in judging others; on the other they are overly sensitive to any perceived injustice. They issue loud protests! To avoid these outcries and charges of injustice, firm and fair rules need to be established and clearly explained. It is best when the students themselves are involved in setting the rules because it encourages responsibility. When they help establish the expected standard of behavior, they better understand and value the rules. It is also a good idea to involve middle school students in discussing appropriate penalties for disobeying rules.

Participating in student government is an activity that offers students opportunities to practice both rule setting and judging the behavior of others. A typical school government will have representatives from every area of the school who constitute a legislative body. A student jury, usually composed of older students, sits in judgment on cases of student misbehavior and recommends disciplinary measures. Because preadolescents are often overly critical of others, they need structured experiences to help them realistically assess situations that cause people to act in less than an ideal manner and to motivate them to show compassion. By developing respect and understanding for others, they improve their own self-concepts and become more aware of the problems and insecurities of others.

Summary

If the library media program is to serve the teachers and students adequately, it is important for the media specialist to understand the background and workings of the school level. Students at the middle school level, and the adults who work with them, face many conflicts. Students need to establish their independence, but they need adults who reassure and guide them. They want to be less reliant on adults, yet they are frightened when there is a lack of mature guidance and established limits. They have an urge to challenge authority, yet depend on authority to provide the direction they need. There is almost constant tugging between being a child and being an adult. A school program must allow students to assume responsibility, but provide a safety net when they fail or falter.

A middle school must provide structure in the school program so that students have the direction and support they need to be willing to try new approaches. It must offer a wide variety of experiences, alternative role models, and opportunities to interact with both their peers and numerous adults. Interaction is particularly important as preadolescents move from a home-dominated environment into a wider community-oriented world. Although students need interaction, they also need quiet times with opportunities for reflection.

Middle school programs must provide variety within structure, which means these programs must be as complex as the students they serve. Students in the ten- to fourteen-year-old age group are trying to find out who they are, to be reassured that they are okay, and to determine just how they fit into this world. Helping them to do so is not an easy job, but it is one which middle school educators tackle every day. These special people have something akin to religious fervor in their belief in the middle school philosophy.

Notes

1. Reflections of William Alexander, *Middle School Journal* 8 (February 1982): 3–7. An interview by editor John H. Lounsbury at the 1981 National Middle School Association's Annual Conference in Miami Beach, Florida.

2. Donald H. Eichhorn, *The Middle School* (New York: Center for Applied Research in Education, 1966), 4.

3. Nicholas P. Georgiady, Jack D. Riegle, and Louis G. Romano, "What Are the Characteristics of the Middle School?" in *The Middle School,* ed. Louis G. Romano, Nicholas P. Georgiady, and James E. Held (Chicago: Nelson-Hall, 1973), 75–84. For an in-depth understanding of middle schools, read issues of *The Middle School Journal,* edited by John Lounsbury.

4. John Dewey, *The School and Society,* rev. ed. (Chicago: University of Chicago Press, 1943), 39.

5. See articles and books about the research of Piaget, for example the following: Mary Carol Day's "Thinking at Piaget's Stage of Operations," *Educational Leadership* 39 (October 1981): 44–45 and Hans G. Furth's *Piaget and Knowledge* (New York: International Universities Press, 1952).

6. Joan Lipsitz, *Growing Up Forgotten: A Review of Research and Programs Concerning Early Adolescence* (Lexington, Mass.: Heath, 1977), 14.

3

Gathering Information about the School

To implement a curriculum-based program, the library media specialist must be well-informed about the local school. As opposed to a public librarian, who must serve a broad population with coverage on seemingly endless topics, a school librarian is really a special librarian with a well-defined population and range of subjects. The scope is narrower but there must be great depth. The purpose of this chapter is to address the depth of knowledge the school librarian needs to have about the school program—particularly a school librarian in a curriculum-based mode.

Gathering this information may be time-consuming for individuals new to a school, but others will already know much of it. Once collected and organized, the information can be updated routinely; for example, by noting changes each time a new state-approved course of study is issued.

A School Survey

The media specialist should know the school program, facility, and surrounding community well enough to describe them to another person and to explain how the various elements are considered in program planning. Figure 3.1 outlines the type of information needed. The following sections of this chapter discuss each item on the survey and suggest ways for a library media specialist to gather information.

The Surrounding Community

The physical environment surrounding the school affects the school program even when most students are bused from other neighborhoods. Unlike a factory or business, a special feeling of ownership generally exists between

FIGURE 3.1 *Checklist for a school information survey*

I. The Surrounding Community

1. Residents
Homogeneous or heterogeneous population
Nationalities represented
Languages spoken on a daily basis
Socioeconomic level and prevalent occupations
Type of housing
Predominant age level

2. Business and Industry
Products
Skills required of workers
Noise or pollution effects
Relationship with school

3. Other Institutions
Libraries
Health care facilities
Government agencies and post office
Educational institutions
Churches

4. Cultural or Recreational Institutions
Galleries or studios
Theaters
Museums
Parks

II. School Facility

1. Physical Layout (windows/light sources and temperature controls, electrical outlets, sound conditions, security features, barriers such as steps or narrow corridors)

2. Usage Layout
Grade level assignments
Special meeting areas and other support service areas
Storage areas

III. School History

1. Notable citizens who attended
2. Changes in the location or design of the structure
3. Changes in student body
4. Past leadership and faculty members

IV. Teachers and Administrators

1. Professional responsibilities
2. Teaching or administrative style
3. Experience with using media
4. Philosophical beliefs about education
5. Out-of-school activities
6. Talents, hobbies, and special skills

V. Parents

1. Socioeconomic status
2. Occupations and skills
3. Housing
4. Nationalities and languages spoken
5. Past association with schools
6. Availability of reading materials in home
7. Leisure-time interests or hobbies

the community and a school within that community. This is one of the reasons school administrators are concerned about maintaining good school/community relations. It is also a reason small communities struggle to retain their schools—because when the schools close, communities often dissolve. Citizens in a community want the schools in their area to be attractive and to have good programs even when they do not have children attending. Neighborhood support is important. Sometimes it is possible to solicit volunteers or gain support for projects from the surrounding community.

On the negative side, knowledge of the area surrounding the school may reveal the need for special security precautions when school is not in session. Material selection may also be influenced by the nature of the community. For example, it may be wise to purchase paperback reading materials in an area with low educational attainment where hardbound books may be unhappy reminders of textbooks. In such locales, homes frequently lack printed materials and students have not developed the practice of caring for them. If so, it may be better to purchase cheaper materials that can be replaced as needed.

Information about the surrounding community can be gathered through a driving or walking tour of the area. Other data-gathering approaches are talking with people in the area who seem receptive to such conversations, reading information on signs or historical markers, and taking note of the types of businesses and institutions in the area. When students live in the area, establish a line of communication by sending an open-ended questionnaire home to parents asking for information about the local area or by involving students in gathering information.

The School Facility

Information about the layout of the school building is necessary to know which material formats can be used effectively and where. For example, light control, availability of electrical outlets, and electrical interference determine the areas where visual projections may be used. Outside noise also impacts the use of audio materials.

A survey of the building reveals areas where equipment can be stored when it is being used over a period of time in one classroom. A floor plan of the building helps identify spaces that can be used for special activities, for satellite collections, or for displays. Complete a building survey by making a large outline map of the school. Visit each space and note the conditions, electrical outlets, storage closets, and cabinets. Label each classroom or learning pod with the appropriate teachers' names.

School History

The history of the school can influence the school program just as much as the neighborhood environment does. An illustrious history is the reason why some schools, even in deteriorating neighborhoods, continue to function with purpose and pride. When a school is publicized as having a number of outstanding alumni, current students may perceive they are also likely to succeed. It heightens esprit de corps.

When a school is well maintained and valued as a community symbol, students and faculty respond. Students are usually interested in finding out information about the school they attend. Involve them in learning more about the origin of the school's name and the names of outstanding citizens who attended.

One way to find information about the school building is to examine parent association publications and scrapbooks, to interview teachers and parents long associated with the school, or to research the school history in the archives of the local newspaper or historical association. Such historical information can be used to strengthen the school and the library media programs.

Parents

No factor influences the success of an educational program more than the parents. What parents do, or fail to do, significantly impacts student performance and attitude. Their actions can either help or hinder the school program. Research data strongly indicate the influence of the parents' ability and educational attainment on their child's performance. Biological factors are critical, but impact also results from the following environmental and familial factors: (1) the availability of educational stimuli in the home environment, (2) parents who model intellectual activities, (3) the occupational status of parents, and (4) the presence of both parents in the home.[1]

Financial factors affect students from the same family differently. In-family factors include such things as how each sibling is treated by the parents, the birth order, spacing between children, cohort differences, and childhood illness.[2] Often a sickly child is overly protected or resented. Many scholars contend the home environment has far more effect on school performance than the characteristics of the school itself. This makes a compelling case for teachers and school librarians to know about the home environment of students.

Information about students' home life is available from a wide assortment of sources. Teachers are usually glad to share any information they have about students' home life, but knowledge about the home environment and family relationships can be also be gained through conversations with parents or through surveys sent to each home. The idea is to obtain background information that is relevant to program planning, not to pry into family relationships. Demographic surveys conducted by the school system and reports available from the school district office will reveal the educational and economic status of represented households. Examining school records and holding professional-level discussions with school counselors and administrators can help a library media specialist obtain adequate background knowledge about students.

The Administration

The school administration is usually key to the success of the school program because administrators affect morale, control the distribution of funds, and set performance expectations. If the principal supports the library media program and expects teachers to work with the librarian to incorporate library activities within each course, it will probably happen. Therefore it is critical for the library media specialist to have a good working relationship with the school administrator.

It is a grave mistake to assume that an administrator understands what the media program contributes to overall school performance. Instead, the library media specialist must sell the program by providing evidence of how library media activities benefit the overall school program and linking library media expenditures to desired school outcomes. Ask teachers to pass along comments to the principal about help they have received from library media services. This is important evidence to the administration that the media program is supporting and furthering school goals.

Support is usually forthcoming when administrators help establish media program priorities, and when they are fully informed about program results. For this reason, there should be a thoughtful and systematic plan for communicating with administrators at both the school and district levels. Adopt a professional stance when making requests, discussing problems, and suggesting alternatives. Be prepared with relevant data and arrange in advance for a meeting time and place. Act as a member of the school team even when budget allocations are not what was requested or when a proposed project is turned down. Nothing is more problematical for an administrator than being faced with an employee's negative behavior.

Get to know each administrator as an individual and find out about his or her educational beliefs and previous professional experiences. Listen carefully to what they say, for personal insights are often revealed in casual remarks. Observe their reactions to different approaches and ideas. Determine whether they find a particular time of day best for problem solving. Do they seem more receptive to proposals and new ideas in the morning or in the afternoon? Learn to interpret their moods and work patterns so that library media matters can be presented at the most opportune time.

The Faculty

School media specialists must become well acquainted with every teacher. Not only must they learn about the instructional strategies and materials each prefers, but they need to know each one personally. Become aware of the out-of-school interests of teachers, because those interests may be useful in library media activities. Understanding each instructor's educational philosophy and preferences makes the cooperative planning process easier and more efficient, yet knowing each teacher as an individual is even more important. The library media specialist needs to ask teachers about past experiences in using media and equipment, about their professional development interests, and about what they expect from media services.

Information about teacher expectations and preferences can be gathered while enjoying a cup of coffee or a shared lunch. If time limitations make that approach unwieldy, ask each teacher to fill out a brief survey form that you can follow with a short personal interview. Another approach is to show a film or video in the media center for each class and while the students are involved confer with the teacher in the media center office.

This strategy allows the library media specialist and the teacher to supervise the students yet to have time for a private conversation. Any meeting with a teacher should be structured to gain as much information as possible in a short period of time. Develop a form on which to record information gained from teachers so that it can be reviewed or updated easily. A sample is provided in Appendix C. Maintain a file for each teacher that includes information collected and copies of joint plans for student activities.

School Goals

School programs should be guided by specific goal statements that are consistent with the educational goals of the school district. Such goal statements are typical of exemplary school programs, so there must be benefits to be derived from following clear goals. Unfortunately, many schools try to develop effective programs without the direction of common and clearly stated goals.

School goals set the pattern for development of a curriculum-based library media program. Get a copy of your school's goals. They will probably be of two types. One type is generic because of the universality of the concern. Such goals include "the development of informed citizens" and "the development of positive self-concepts." Even though similar goals are listed for many school programs, the methods used to reach those goals will differ from school to school because each school is unique. The second type of goal is a response to local needs. Locally driven goals reflect current curricular emphases or inadequacies. Examples of local concerns might be a sudden plunge in student scores on work with fractions, a suspected increase in drug use by the school population, or an influx of foreign-born students. Both types of goals should be reflected in objectives and activities set forth for the library media program.

School Policies and Procedures

Most public schools are hierarchical organizations with rules and procedures originating at an upper level, usually at the district and state level. Media specialists need to know those policies, particularly the ones that impact media services. Similarly, practitioners in private schools must know the priorities and practices endorsed by their school governing board. Media-related policies include administrative functions such as budgeting, expenditure of funds, record retention, scheduling, inventorying, securing copyright clearances, circulating equipment/materials, providing in-service training, and handling reconsideration requests.

Information about school policies can be obtained by reviewing available documents and questioning the appropriate administrators or central office personnel. Most districts have a policy manual that contains the rules and procedures approved by the local board of education. An updated copy of this manual should be shelved in each library's professional collection and the media specialist should be familiar with its content and organization. Any plans made for the media program must be in accord with school and district policies.

The Instructional Program

Perhaps the most important and relevant data source in planning the library media program is the school's instructional program. Becoming familiar with the instructional program requires examining instructional outlines, test data, lesson plans, textbooks, library resources, and supplementary teaching materials.

Instructional Outline

Most school districts have a written statement of instructional intent called a curriculum guide. This guide outlines how certain required content will be taught. Local curriculum committees decide the pace, sequence, strategies, and resources to be used. Usually, the minimum required instruction in each discipline is established at the state level and the local committee uses the state outline.

Information Power: Guidelines for School Library Media Programs encourages the media specialist to be involved as a member of the curriculum committee.[3] After all, who better knows the resources that are available? Unfortunately, in some schools the library media specialist has been excluded from making decisions that affect classrooms, even when the librarian volunteers to serve on the committee. Whether involved in decision making or not, the library media specialist must stay abreast of the decisions that are made and should have copies of all curriculum outlines in the media center's professional collection.

A library media specialist should be aware of what is being taught in each subject at each grade level. One way to keep a record of the topics being taught is to create a large chart that can be posted on the wall of the media center. Some library media specialists prefer to keep such information in a loose-leaf notebook because it is so easy to update or change. See Figure 3.2 for an example of a topic chart or an annual survey of topics by grade level.

After developing a list of topics, find out the objectives related to each topic. Many objectives are similar across grade levels and from one subject to the other. When this is so, it offers opportunities to use multigrade groups or to help several teachers teach a skill or concept even though the teachers are teaching different subjects.

Identifying objectives that are both instructional objectives and standardized test objectives can also help simplify the teaching task. For example, the following objectives were listed on a language arts curriculum guide, as content objectives for a standardized test, and on a media skills scope and sequence list:

1. Include who, what, when, where, and why in a message.
2. Determine word meaning from context.
3. Determine the main idea that is implied in a selection.
4. Recognize irrelevant statements in a passage.
5. Choose the correct meaning from contextual clues.
6. Select and use different sections of a book.
7. Distinguish fact from opinion or fact from fantasy.

FIGURE 3.2 *Sample survey of topics by grade level*

Grade 6
Teaching Team: Richardson, Williams & Cabell   Pod: A

SUBJECT	September	October	November	December	January	February	March	April	May
Math	Measurement	Word Problems	Fractions		Decimal Equivalents	Factors	Prime Numbers		Geometry
Science	Human-Body	Mixtures & Solutions		Energy & Matter		Weather	Solar System		Space
Social Studies	Canada	Canada	Map & Globe Skills	U.S. Ethnic Groups	Australia		Latin & South America		
Language Arts	Compound Sentences	Oral Reports / Fact & Opinion	Inferences / Almanac		Outlining Dictated Notes Editing		Fables	Tall Tales	Imagery & Poetry

Grade 7
Teaching Team: Fletcher, Jamison & McDonald   Pod: C

SUBJECT	September	October	November	December	January	February	March	April	May
Math	Relations & Properties	Measurement		Geometric Relations	Two Operation Problems		Percents; Metric System		
Science	Sound, Heat & Light as Change Agents		Elements & Compounds		Cells & Body Systems		Drug Education	Scientific Process	
Social Studies	Western Europe	Europe	Eastern Europe		Cultural Expression		Africa		Inter-dependence of Nations
Language Arts	Interviewing / Notetaking	Newspapers	Propaganda		Current Events	Elements of Fiction		Mythology	Common Forms & Labels

Being aware of common objectives simplifies the task of planning effective instruction.

Lesson Plans

It helps when the library media specialist has access to each teacher's lesson plans because they provide information about teaching strategies, grouping arrangements, pacing of content, and media preferences. Even if teachers are reluctant to share their plans, a skillful library media specialist can determine what is taking place in the classroom by being aware of the textbook content, talking with students about classroom activities, observing class displays, and reviewing requests for materials and equipment.

Test Results

Analyze a profile of available test scores to gain useful information about areas of instructional need. While caution should be taken not to compare one class with another or one student with another, analyzing student performance will indicate instructional objectives that are not being addressed effectively. It may be that these needs can be addressed through activities in the media center. For example, the faculty of one school in which student listening performance dropped dramatically decided to set up six listening centers in the media center that would be used for delivery of course content. The teachers taped content related to student requirements and the students had to listen in order to gain needed information. Through increased use of auditory learning followed by frequent testing and feedback, student performance improved.

Test data can be helpful in designing media services and activities. First, the library media specialist can prepare students for those portions of the tests related to information retrieval and use of resources. Knowledge of the standardized test objectives also helps the media specialist determine whether the existing media collection supports instruction adequately. Third, test data help target instructional objectives in need of special attention, as in the example of listening behavior cited above.

Textbook Survey

Following an overall review of curriculum or instructional objectives, the second step in surveying the instructional program is to review the textbooks being used. Although many educational leaders continue to bemoan the reliance teachers place on textbooks, which are often criticized as superficial and pedantic, they continue to be the basis for much of the teaching that goes on. Obviously, then, their content must be reviewed if a media specialist is to know what is happening in the school program.

It is not necessary for a library media specialist to read each text word by word, but a technical review of each title should be made (see Figure 3.3). A technical review will reveal the book's coverage, approach, arrangement, scope, and special features. Such a review can be quickly accomplished by surveying the table of contents, index, illustrations, and special features. Next, note the resource list at the end of each chapter. Later you can check the

FIGURE 3.3 *Checklist for technically reviewing a textbook*

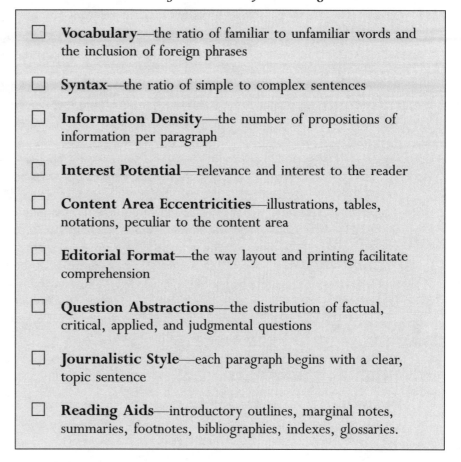

☐ **Vocabulary**—the ratio of familiar to unfamiliar words and the inclusion of foreign phrases

☐ **Syntax**—the ratio of simple to complex sentences

☐ **Information Density**—the number of propositions of information per paragraph

☐ **Interest Potential**—relevance and interest to the reader

☐ **Content Area Eccentricities**—illustrations, tables, notations, peculiar to the content area

☐ **Editorial Format**—the way layout and printing facilitate comprehension

☐ **Question Abstractions**—the distribution of factual, critical, applied, and judgmental questions

☐ **Journalistic Style**—each paragraph begins with a clear, topic sentence

☐ **Reading Aids**—introductory outlines, marginal notes, summaries, footnotes, bibliographies, indexes, glossaries.

school's collection to see which recommended resources it contains. Make notes about the authors whose works are included in the text and the types of literature used as excerpts. Similar works, or other works by the same authors, can be featured in library media displays, included in library media activities, or simply routed to classrooms to encourage leisure reading.

In addition to informing the media specialist about course content, technically reviewing a textbook suggests whether the content and reading level are appropriate for the students. A readability index is based on word and sentence length, but those are not the only characteristics that can make informational materials difficult to digest. Giordano illustrates this point with an income tax form.[4] The tax manual has appropriate readability level for the average reader if word and sentence length are the only measures used, but other factors such as density of information make a tax form difficult to comprehend. In seeking to determine the degree of difficulty of text material, ask the following questions:

1. Are there many unfamiliar words?

2. Are foreign phrases included?

3. Is most sentence construction simple or complex?

4. Is there more than one idea per paragraph?

5. Is the content relevant and interesting to the student?

6. Are illustrations, tables, and notations appropriate to the content?

7. Do the layout and printing style facilitate comprehension?

8. Are questions sprinkled throughout to encourage review?

9. Does each paragraph begin with a clear topic sentence?

10. Are reading aids, such as outlines, summaries, footnotes, and indexes provided?

Textbooks are selected for a mass audience and the audience profile might not match the students in any one school. Of course once a set of textbooks has been purchased, a school is not going to discard them; however, the library media specialist can help ameliorate many problems associated with adopted textbooks. For example, if there are many unfamiliar words but no glossary or definitions in the text, the media specialist could help the teacher develop a glossary, laminate it, and insert it in the back of each book. This simple action can increase the usefulness of materials owned by the school. With today's limited budgets and increased costs this is increasingly important.

Collection Analysis

Essential responsibilities for library media specialists are organizing, maintaining, and circulating a library collection. However, a more important responsibility is to ensure that library resources are well utilized. To do this, the library media specialist must be familiar with items in the collection and must correlate the collection with the curriculum. This implies that the media specialist must know (1) what materials are in the collection, (2) how the materials correlate with the school program, and (3) whether and how teachers are using those materials. Getting maximum use from each item in a collection requires analyzing the collection thoroughly and assessing the strength and weakness of each item in light of the curriculum.

Collection correlation may be done in different ways. For skill development subjects such as language arts and mathematics, it may be best to correlate materials with specific instructional objectives. This pattern is useful because teachers often need to remediate or provide enrichment for students in a specific skill. In these subjects, teachers may need materials that address a specific skill, not just material that generally addresses language arts, listening, or sounds.

To correlate a collection with instructional units or topics, the media specialist does not have to go through each item but can ask teachers and students to help. When a collection review project is carefully planned, students will see the correlation of materials and objectives as somewhat like a game, but it can be both a learning experience for them and a time saver for the library media specialist. Teachers can also be given a form and asked to identify the instructional objectives covered in the items they check out. Over a period of time this cooperative approach will result in an analysis of most of the collection. If necessary, however, the library media specialist can complete the task alone. Once the collection has been correlated with the curriculum's instructional objectives, staying abreast will only be needed as new things are added to the collection or as teaching objectives are altered or added.

Supplementary Materials Review

A record of materials that teachers use to supplement or augment textbooks can either be drawn from lesson plans or compiled throughout the year as items are checked out. The advantage of identifying materials through lesson plans is that it gives one a better idea of how the materials are being used in the classroom. However, some teachers do not have lesson plans for the entire year when school begins, but develop them for an upcoming unit while teaching the current unit. In this case it will be necessary to gather information throughout the year. This can be advantageous in that the yearlong communication may create a closer relationship between the teacher and the media specialist.

Information obtained from a survey of supplementary materials may suggest media services that will help improve instruction, such as

1. locating materials in outside collections,
2. routing pertinent professional information to teaching teams,
3. alerting teachers to forthcoming programs and telecasts related to their lessons,
4. developing materials that cannot be commercially obtained.

Recommending and securing supplementary teaching resources are important activities that support the instructional program; these responsibilities should not be taken lightly. Recommending resources can validate the role of an instructional resource person. Identifying and locating outside resources are skills in which a library media specialist is trained and many teachers are not; therefore, it is important for the media specialist to lead or assist in this activity.

Having completed the six steps of an instructional review, the library media specialist should have a clear understanding of the purpose and parameters of the teaching program. The next step, then, is planning library media services and activities.

Summary

Armed with an understanding of the school community, aware of the facility characteristics, knowledgeable about the school program, and informed about student performance, a library media specialist has the background information needed to plan with teachers. As such planning takes place, the library media specialist will be amazed by the change in faculty perceptions of his or her role. This transition has been observed many times. When teachers know the librarian is aware of what they are trying to do and is interested in the particulars of their classrooms, it establishes different working relationships. Certainly gaining such knowledge takes time, but the benefits greatly outweigh the effort required.

Just as one phase of the planning process impacts others, becoming knowledgeable about the instructional program impacts other areas of library operation. Knowing what and how subjects are taught sharpens selection skills. Acquisitions will be more closely matched with needs. An instructional survey such as the one outlined in this chapter is useful both in promoting collaborative projects among faculty and in communicating with parents and administrators.

Notes

1. Kevin Marjoribanks, "Occupational Situs, Family Learning Environment and Children's Academic Achievement," *Alberta Journal of Educational Research* 24 (June 1983): 110–22.

2. Robert B. McCall, "Environmental Effects on Intelligence: The Forgotten Realm of Discontinuous Nonshared Within-Family Factors," *Child Development* 54 (1983): 408–15.

3. American Association of School Librarians and the Association for Educational Communications and Technology, *Information Power: Guidelines for School Library Media Programs* (Chicago: American Library Association, 1988), 39.

4. Gerard Giordano, "How Complex Is Your Textbook?" *The Clearinghouse* 55 (April 1982): 369–73.

Planning a Curriculum-Based Program

Planning the library media program requires making decisions in advance about what services and activities are needed based on the data at hand. Unfortunately, most school media specialists report they do not plan an annual program, but only plan intermittently for special activities. As a result, these specialists spend most of their time responding to others instead of implementing a plan designed to achieve specific objectives. By the end of the school year, these library media specialists are frustrated because they have little evidence of accomplishment despite all their hard work. How much better they would feel if they had a planned media program that supported school goals and would enable them to demonstrate the effectiveness of the library media program.

Many people avoid planning because it is a complex and time-consuming task. In addition, a program plan is best accomplished through group process, involving representatives of the organization that will be affected. Group process is also complex and time-consuming. Perhaps it is understandable why many library media specialists find reasons to avoid planning an annual program. One intent of this chapter is to endorse planning as essential for a truly effective program and to present a simple planning model that can be used.

The Planning Model

Planning models have been presented in many formats, including the three stages and nine steps shown in the original edition of this book. While it is useful to use a planning model, at least when you first begin to plan an annual program, it does not matter which model is used. Any organized and systematic method can guide the planning process and also be used as an informational tool to inform others about the actions and decisions being taken.

A systematic process is one in which actions initiated in one step impact or trigger others. Let us use as an example a school goal "to develop students who are capable information retrievers." The rationale for this goal is traced to the increase in available information, the complexity of ideas, and the nature of today's world that requires changing lifestyles, careers, and location. An analysis of test results and teacher reports suggests many sixth grade students lack skill in reading and developing graphs and charts—an important information format. During the planning process, this need is judged a priority for the skills instruction service. Alternative solutions to the problem of poor student performance in this area are generated, considered, and selected.

One activity selected is to establish a graph and chart center in the library where students can be scheduled as individuals or small groups for a variety of related learning experiences. To make this activity available, several things may be required. Action may be taken to secure additional commercial resources, to plan instructional activities with the sixth grade teaching team, or to recruit parent volunteers to help develop teaching materials from charts and graphs found in newspapers and magazines. It is probable that many actions will be taken, some in advance of the school year and some as the school year progresses. A related activity, part of the instructional consulting service, is planning an in-service meeting on visual organizers to heighten the faculty's awareness of how to present information effectively through charts, graphs, and other visual devices. Plans are made jointly with the school computer lab to stress instruction in spreadsheets with particular emphasis on using the application program to develop charts and graphs. Evaluation strategies must be identified to assess students' skills in a more specific manner than the standardized test results which first suggested the need for additional attention to the area of charts and graphs. This example should make it evident how one action triggers another in the planning cycle.

The model presented in the 1988 book has been greatly simplified for this edition. The original nine steps are now presented as the following four planning phases:

1. Gathering information related to need,
2. Setting priorities for services and activities,
3. Establishing a plan of action, and
4. Evaluating the services and activities to determine how well the plan is working.

Analyzing the evaluative data gathered in the fourth phase will suggest changes that need to be made, which brings you back to phase one—a move that underscores the cyclical nature of the planning process.

Within each of the four planning phases there are enabling actions that must be taken by the planners. For example phase three, "establishing a plan of action," will include a host of decisive actions such as generating alternatives, specifying who will do what, determining when each thing will happen, and securing appropriate space and resources. A more detailed planning process usually presents these enabling steps.

Following the suggested four-phase planning outline will not result in look-alike library media programs because the starting point for each plan is different. This is only logical. A library media program should mirror the characteristics of a school program, school population, faculty, and community. All schools are different, so the reflected library media program will be different. The unique combination of strengths, style, and preferences of the librarian also contribute to making one program differ from another. Just as a teacher's personality shapes classroom events, the library media specialist's style imprints the media program. An important fundamental in curriculum-based programming is respect for these differences.

Some library media specialists are uneasy if they are not doing what others are doing. Yet the variety in program activities is the number one reason why directing a library media program is so much fun. A classroom does not offer the same amount of flexibility and variation because of time requirements, prescribed curriculum, and focus on textbooks. Library media specialists have a real advantage. However, if what goes on in the library media center does not relate to needs of the school program and seems not to fit the students' characteristics, library media activities may have little value in the eyes of others in the school community. When library media services and activities are isolated from the school program, teachers often feel out of touch with the library media specialist. In this era of site-based school management, such feelings of separation have led some school councils to decide the school no longer needed a library media specialist. With this caveat given, it's back to planning!

The first phase in the planning process, gathering information related to the school program, was addressed in the first two chapters of this book. The remainder of this chapter focuses on phase two, establishing priorities, and the group process for carrying it out. Phase three, establishing a plan of action, is explained and illustrated in Chapters 5 through 7. Tools to use in the fourth phase, program evaluation, are provided in the last chapter.

Program Priorities

In establishing priorities, the first issue to be addressed is that of services. School library media programs generally provide the following traditional services: resource management, reference, literature enrichment, and skill instruction. Today, many programs also offer production services and instructional consulting, which is a service directed to teachers and intended to help them improve classroom instruction. By definition, services are broad categories of actions undertaken for the benefit and enjoyment of the school community.

Information Power lists twenty-two services that were found in library media programs judged as high-service programs in an analysis of data collected by the U.S. Department of Education.[1] The services listed in this study are more specific than the categories named in the previous paragraph. The list includes things such as:

Coordinates library skills instruction with classroom instruction.

Assists curriculum committee in selecting appropriate materials and media program activities for resource units and curriculum guides.

Helps individual teachers to coordinate media program activities and resources with subject areas, units, and textbooks.

Provides technical assistance to teachers in the production of materials.

These services can all be categorized as instructional consulting because they are directed to the faculty and are intended to benefit student instruction. It does not matter whether service priorities are based on the twenty-two services listed in *Information Power* or on the categories previously mentioned. The important point is that services must be prioritized because it is not possible to do everything, and setting service priorities establishes a framework for further planning.

Priorities for the library media program should reflect school program values. Examine the three circles in Figure 4.1. Each circle illustrates the service priorities of a different library media program. Can you determine the priorities of each school program from examining the priorities established for each library media program?

One program emphasizes service to faculty, another emphasizes student research, one illustrates the importance of production services while another fails to show it. The pie graphs are simplistic for a purpose. They illustrate program priorities because they show what has been chosen and what has not, and they also suggest the time allocation.

While the results of the prioritizing process can be presented in a simple format, the decisions underlying the priority setting process can be very complex and require careful discussion and consideration. Once the services have been prioritized and some general time allocations made, attention must be given to prioritizing the activities to be included within each service.

FIGURE 4.1 *Three programs with different priorities*

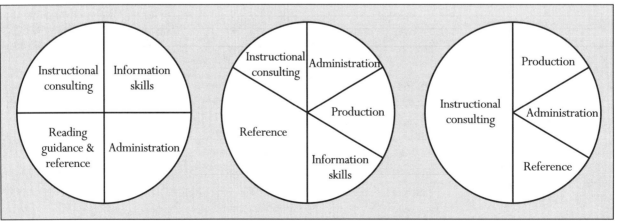

Activities are events that give substance to each service. For example, activities in a literature enrichment service might include book talks, book discussion groups, author visits, special displays, or viewing plays based on classic novels. There may be only one or two activities constituting a service or more than a hundred. While two schools might offer the same media services, and even have similar time allocations, the activities will differ. Not only will they differ from program to program, but within a given program the activities will be different from year to year.

These program-defining decisions can be made by a library media specialist acting alone, but the program will be stronger if decisions are made cooperatively by members selected from the school community. Planning with others does require more time, and perhaps some frustration; however, the results are usually better, and the process builds understanding and support for the media program.

Library Media Committee Involvement

The best way to establish priorities for the library media program is through deliberations of a committee that represents the total school community. The committee should include faculty representatives, administrators, media professionals, parents, a public librarian, and student leaders. Having a representative group establish priorities enables the library media specialist to provide activities that the school community desires. Members of this committee should be appointed or invited to serve by the school principal. At least one school administrator should be among the planning group. Appendix A contains information helpful to those establishing a media committee for the first time.

In addition to setting priorities for the library media program, the library media committee can act as a selection committee, consider challenges to materials, and recommend policies or procedures. The members also serve as a conduit for information, which flows in to make certain the program responds to the total school community and flows out to inform members of the school community about the media program and its benefits. This group may be called the media committee, program planning committee, or whatever you choose, but their meetings should be structured and scheduled in advance. Cooperative decision making underscores the principle that the media program belongs to everyone in the school and that it reflects their needs, interests, and ideas. Naturally this principle also means the committee is not expected to rubber-stamp the wishes and actions of the library media specialist.

Background information should be distributed to committee members in advance of any meeting. When the meeting is to identify program priorities for the coming year, the background information should include a list of the previous year's services and activities. The committee should also have the results of a needs assessment questionnaire in which a sample of teachers and students rated the value of activities from the past year. This information will help establish priorities for those that should be retained or added in the coming year. Information furnished to the committee provides the basis for discussion. They need evidence of services and activities that successfully supported school goals, resulted in improved student performance, helped teachers improve instruction, and encouraged student use of materials.

Several good suggestions are made in a planning guide developed by the American Association of School Librarians to help library media specialists implement *Information Power* guidelines. One suggestion is to designate a recorder for the planning meetings. A recorder keeps up with the committee's ideas and records them on a blackboard, transparency, or flip chart.[2]

Following a general discussion of last year's services and activities, the group must decide upon those for the coming year. As chairperson of the committee, the library media specialist leads members to a consensus about which services and activities are most needed. One strategy to use in reaching consensus is to have each member of the committee rank order the services according to importance and then compile the results. If there are wide discrepancies, further discussion and a second rank ordering may be needed. When there is general agreement on the services that should be included, gain consensus on the percentage of time that should be spent on each service. Next, repeat the process to select and prioritize activities.

Priorities established by the committee will guide the media specialist in planning activities prior to and during the coming year. This process ensures a relationship with the school community. It helps ensure the library media program will promote the school's goals, making the program consistent with professional guidelines developed twenty years ago. Those guidelines state that the media program exists

> to further the purposes formulated by the school or district of which it is an integral part, and its quality is judged by its effectiveness in achieving program purposes. A media program represents a combination of resources that includes people, materials, machines, facilities, and environments, as well as purposes and processes. The combination of these program components and the emphasis given to each of them derive from the needs of the specific educational program. The more purposeful and effective the mix, and the more sensitively it responds to the curriculum and the learning environment, the better the media program.[3]

Summary

Effective library media programs are based on school goals and reflect the interests and needs of the school community. Such programs rarely occur without advance planning, and planning proceeds more smoothly when a systematic process is used. When planning involves a representative group of the school community, the plan is more likely to be effective. The group process develops knowledgeable proponents for the services and activities and serves as a pipeline for information.

There are many planning outlines. The one presented in this chapter involves four phases. It begins with gathering information about the school program. This information is used as a pattern for designing the library media program. The process, best undertaken through a representative planning group, engages the representatives in establishing program priorities. Service priorities and suggested time allotments are decided on first; next comes prioritizing of activities. With these program outlines and working with other faculty, a library media specialist can develop an action plan and evaluative strategies.

Notes

1. American Association of School Librarians and Association for Educational Communications and Technology, *Information Power: Guidelines for School Library Media Programs* (Chicago: American Library Association, 1988), 116.

2. American Association of School Librarians, *A Planning Guide for Information Power: Guidelines for School Library Media Programs* (Chicago: American Library Association, 1988), 13.

3. American Association of School Librarians and Association for Educational Communications and Technology, *Media Programs: District and School* (Chicago: American Library Association, 1975), 4.

5

Planning
Curriculum-Based
Activities

Dean John Lounsbury, in the epigraph of this book, identifies the two tasks of a middle school program as human development and skill development. Curriculum-based programs address both. In this chapter and the next, attention will be directed toward skill development and its counterpart, content acquisition.

Curriculum Map

Developing curriculum-based library media activities requires an overall understanding of the courses, topics, and perspectives that comprise or influence the instructional program. This information is gained by

- analyzing the courses of study and curriculum guides that outline instruction,
- reviewing the textbooks for content,
- noting lesson plans to see what is happening in classrooms, and
- reviewing test data for evidence of instructional gaps.

Some educators call such a curriculum review an audit or curriculum mapping.[1] While it may not be possible to complete a curriculum map for all courses or grades in a single year, the process should be started and a schedule developed for completing the activity. One schedule for collecting such instructional data would be to adopt a grade-by-grade system; another would be to use a subject-by-subject approach.

Since all five data sources for a curriculum map—courses of study, curriculum guides, textbooks, lesson plans, and tests—are regularly revised, regular updates will be necessary. Usually course of study revision and textbook adoption occur in cycles of five to seven years, which means that substantial changes will be infrequent. Routine changes in lesson plans are likely to involve updating content, incorporating a new resource, or adopting a different strategy. As with any collection, the curriculum database is easier to maintain than it is to originate.

The overview of topics to be addressed during the year, such as the example shown in Chapter 2, provides the background information a library media specialist needs to discuss the instructional program intelligently with teachers, and it furnishes the information needed to plan media center activities. This overview assists in teacher-to-teacher communication because it reminds everyone about what is being addressed at any given time across the instructional program. A curriculum map is a more detailed overview of instruction that promotes sharing of materials or jointly planned projects among faculty members.

A good example of the kind of cooperation that is spawned through a curriculum map is shown in the following illustration:

> The sixth grade teaching team has arranged for the editor of a local newspaper to critique a class-developed newsletter and to share his reporting experiences. The media specialist knows about the plan because of cooperative planning and advises the eighth grade teachers who are teaching a unit on mass media advertising. The eighth grade teachers ask about getting the editor to discuss newspaper advertising with their students and to assess the mock-up advertisements they have created.

For this cooperation to happen, someone must serve as a clearinghouse so that teachers of one grade level know what the others have planned. Despite good intentions, most teaching teams operate independently and with little communication. The centralized position of the media program within the school makes coordination an appropriate responsibility for the media specialist.

Having a master schedule of instruction also results in more comprehensive use of materials. It is a shameful lost opportunity when a film or video that is rented for one class is discovered to have great relevance to a topic being studied in another grade or subject, but it was returned before the second potential use was discovered. Using it twice doubles the value of the expenditure.

Cooperative Planning

Armed with a curriculum map and the committee's priorities, the library media specialist is ready to develop activity plans with teachers. At this point, planning times must be arranged. Middle schools provide ideal settings for media specialists to serve as instructional consultants because regularly scheduled planning times bring all the members of the instructional team together. Middle school teachers are accustomed to cooperative planning and the majority of school administrators expect the media specialist to function as part of the instructional team.

If the practice of cooperative planning is not already established, it must be begun. Often this is easier said than done, because each person believes there is time for nothing more. To initiate the habit of cooperative planning, it may be necessary to use some of the change strategies described in Chapter 1. An easy way to get teachers involved in cooperative planning is for the library media specialist to start attending each grade-level meeting or teaching-team planning period. Routine attendance is important in order to stay abreast of events, but it is not necessary to attend every one.

When the library media specialist is well-informed about the school's instructional program and has the opportunity to plan with teachers, he or she can support and strengthen classroom instruction through a broad scope of activities which include, but are not limited to, those shown in Figure 5.1.

A principal who has been made aware of the range of activities that can be developed to enrich instruction will probably see to it that those services are made available.

The Benefits of Collaboration

Things go better when teachers and the media specialist work together because the team effort increases individual achievements. While these two professionals have different responsibilities, they have a shared concern for student achievement. The teacher's primary concern is with the teaching technique; the effectiveness of instructional materials is secondary. The media specialist is concerned first with the effective utilization of materials and secondly with the technique being employed. It is not a matter of which is more important; instead, it is more like the chicken and the egg—hard to tell which came first!

Instructional Design

In developing curriculum-based activities, the media specialist combines knowledge of the school's instructional program with an understanding of the instructional design process to communicate with teachers about classroom instruction in a structured manner. As they discuss objectives, strategies, materials, and evaluation, using the instructional design framework helps categorize information about the teaching plan. Bill Hug's book, *Instructional Design and the Media Program,* is a classic guide in this process. He reminds media specialists of their challenge to work with teachers to incorporate all the advantages of available media in their instructional plans.

Even if the teacher does not know fundamentals of the instructional design process, it is possible for a media specialist to use it to communicate with teachers "to improve the teaching-learning process."[2] An example of such a situation is illustrated in the following conversation between a fictitious librarian and classroom teacher.

Teacher: "Next month I will be teaching the westward expansion unit and I need some new materials or new ideas."

Librarian: "Yes, I read your revised outline of the unit. Perhaps we can plan some small group sessions in map skills and use of

FIGURE 5.1 *Ways to support classroom instruction*

Recommend media for specific purposes.

Evaluate the effectiveness of various formats.

Reinforce student's skill acquisition.

Identify examples in literature related to classroom exercises or content.

Provide professional information to assist teachers in improving teaching skills.

Provide course-related information to help teachers remain up-to-date.

Provide in-service programs in equipment utilization.

Relate textbook content to information in reference books and outside information sources.

Recommend supplementary materials for use in classroom activities.

Obtain online information about human resources.

Alter or produce materials when needed.

Offer staff development programs to promote better utilization of materials.

Inform teachers about copyright provisions and decisions.

Suggest ways and resources that will guide students to materials that extend or enrich classroom learning.

Infuse information skills into coursework so that students have the skills they need to effectively acquire and use information.

Provide instructional resources cited in textbooks.

Maintain and circulate equipment for available materials.

Correlate library books with classroom topics to encourage outside reading.

Secure needed media not available in the school collection.

an historical atlas to go along with the unit. I'd like to know more about your plans for teaching the unit. Tell me, what do you expect the students to be able to do by the end of the unit? Will they be expected to retrace the routes of the explorers or only to associate the explorer's name with the region discovered?"

The media specialist continues using considerations in the design process to question the teacher in a way that elicits specific expectations. When the librarian asks what the students are expected to be able to do at the completion of the learning activity, she wants to know the instructional objectives. Knowing what is intended will suggest a range of alternative ways to deliver instruction and practice. This enables the media specialist to suggest appropriate materials. By the end of the conversation, the media specialist will understand what the teacher intends to happen and will be in tune with the teacher's ideas. This clarification process is similar to a reference interview when the library user has not clearly identified the type and amount of information needed.

Teachers who write clearly stated outcomes or objectives make it easier for others to know their intentions. The verb in the objective elaborates the degree of learning. Will the student be expected to classify, to define, to discuss, to list, or to choose? Each verb suggests different materials and evaluative techniques. If the student is expected to "compare" something, the media specialist knows there must be two or more samples. "Select" or "choose" generally indicates more than two samples should be available. "Define" requires more of the learner than to distinguish between or among choices. The precision with which an objective is stated makes it easier to understand the teacher's intent and to aptly correlate existing materials, to suggest appropriate strategies, or to enhance the lesson through acquisition of new resources or production of locally designed items.

Certification requirements in most states now require library media specialists to be competent in using the instructional design process. Ancillary understanding is knowledge about learning theory, needs assessment techniques, task analysis, learning taxonomies, instructional theories, various presentation modes, and media attributes.

Instructional Activity Plans

When planning an instructional activity, certain elements of a good lesson plan should be included. Answering the following questions will generate those needed elements:

- What is the purpose of this instruction?
- How does the topic relate to what students already know?
- What should be done to interest students in the content?
- How will the content be delivered?
- What will the students do?
- Is the activity appropriate to the age of the learners?
- Should the learners be grouped? If so, how?
- Are the materials appropriate to the age of the learners?
- Will all learners use the same materials?
- What materials will be used to vary instruction?
- How will students be evaluated?
- What level of performance will be accepted?
- How will students be remediated?

Any instructional plan that answers these questions can be shaped into the following five stages of good instruction:

1. introducing the topic,
2. presenting the content,
3. providing guided practice,
4. evaluating learning, and
5. remediation, or extended practice, or enrichment.

Instructional Concerns

In planning instructional activities, the teacher and the media specialist are concerned with devising the most effective strategies and using the most precise resources. These are complex and difficult decisions, particularly in the middle school where there is so much diversity in student development, interests, and achievement. The instructional events planned by teachers and the library media specialist may take place in the library media center, in the classroom, or in some other designated area. Regardless of where the teaching and learning take place, all members of the instructional planning team are concerned with effectiveness.

Materials

Content must be presented in a manner, format, and pace that makes it possible for the students to learn. Good design and appropriate pairing of learner and material result in effective presentations; in other words, good products need to be properly matched to the student.

An illustration of this concern is realizing the contribution of motion in facilitating understanding of a process. When people *see* the process unfold from beginning to end, it is much easier to understand how one step leads to another and how one stage affects the other. This is as true for the steel manufacturing process as it is for the hatching of an egg. However, if the learner is not able to comprehend the vocabulary or is not able to put the visual in perspective, then learning will not take place. Good instruction requires both an appropriate level of content and an appropriate format.

In some instances a media attribute is a necessity and sometimes it is only an added feature. Part of the responsibility of an instructional consultant is to help determine when certain features are essential and when they are just an added bonus. Those extra features are fine when they genuinely add to the effectiveness of instruction, but added features are educational extravagance. These days of tight budgets require us to get the best use from each dollar that is expended. A curriculum-based library media program helps the school get the most effective instructional materials for the least amount of money.

Media specialists are involved in finding or producing materials that differ in format but address similar content objectives. It is important to accommodate different learning style preferences. Sometimes this accommodation requires developing materials locally. Because of the time and effort this action requires, local materials should not be the first choice.

Several points need to be considered before embarking on local production. Kent Gustafson and Fred Knirk discuss these considerations in their book, *Instructional Technology.* An adapted chart is found in Figure 5.2 which you can use with teachers in deciding if local production is the path to follow.

Evaluation

Evaluation is a critically important part of instruction, and thus a concern of each member of the instructional team. The library media specialist is interested in the outcome of instruction regardless of where it takes place. When the library media specialist teaches students directly, she needs an evaluation plan. Information about student performance on tasks in the media center needs to be relayed to the classroom teachers.

On occasion, the media specialist will provide instruction, furnish the teacher with test items, and ask the teacher to include those items on a classroom test. Even if the specialist was not involved in direct instruction, it is likely he was involved in furnishing materials, and therefore, needs to know how well students learned.

FIGURE 5.2 *Matching materials to content: Steps in the process*

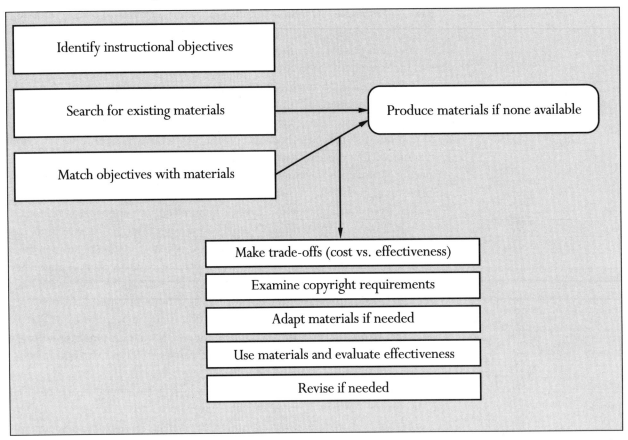

Adapted from: Frederick G. Knirk and Kent L. Gustafson, *Instructional Technology: A Systematic Approach in Education* (New York: Holt, Rinehart, and Winston, 1986).

The teacher and the media specialist need to analyze student performance together. The teacher will look closely at the effectiveness of the teaching strategy and the instructional activities, while the media specialist will be more concerned with the effectiveness and appropriateness of the materials used in instruction. Together they will try to answer such questions as those shown in Figure 5.3. The answers to these and similar questions will guide the teacher and media specialist in making the instructional activity more effective.

Variation

The results of an evaluation can help the instructional team vary an activity for those who did not learn the first time. A variation or improvement may be helpful for all students, even if only a few did not learn through the original approach. However, the joint analysis and revision procedures are important for effective instruction.

When media specialists plan with teachers, they should be prepared to suggest additional supplementary materials, more effective ways to use certain materials, and variations in technique. An example of the way in

FIGURE 5.3 *Evaluation considerations*

Did the students perform as expected?

Which students did not do well? Why?

What are the common characteristics of those who did poorly?

Which parts of the materials appear to have been effective?

Did the instructional material match the objectives?

Was the terminology too difficult or too vague?

Was the print size adequate?

Was the pacing of the material too fast or too slow?

Did the illustrations clarify or confuse the content?

Were there adequate examples?

Did the examples relate to the students' interests or lives?

Was the material well-organized or were the learners groping for direction?

Were there outside distractions that inhibited the effectiveness of the presentation?

Was the setting conducive to use of the material?

Did the equipment operate correctly?

Could the students hear the sound adequately?

Was there adequate distinction between colors?

which the library media specialist can help a teacher devise more effective learning situations is shown in the vignette below.

> The teacher has decided to use a set of teaching pictures with his class; although he is aware it is not a good medium for full class instruction, he does not know of anything else that provides the needed content. The media specialist knows that similar scenes are included in a slide presentation, although its title does not suggest the relevant content. Because the media specialist is familiar with each product in the collection and knows the instructional intent, she can suggest it to the teacher.

The suggestion can be made verbally during a planning session, by dropping a note in the teacher's school mailbox, or by setting up the slide projector on a cart and rolling it to the teacher's room for an after-school preview. Too often the outcome of such a situation is not a satisfied teacher equipped to do his best, but something like the following scenario:

> A teacher enters the media center looking for a filmstrip on Chinese culture to use with a sixth grade class. The materials catalog does not have anything listed under the headings "China" or "Far Eastern Cultures." The teacher returns to the classroom complaining that the media center never has what is needed for instruction.

However, a media specialist well versed in the content of the collection might have been able to suggest a section of a videotape on the process of papermaking that also featured typical housing in the Far East.

The library media specialist functions as an instructional consultant, striving to help all teachers succeed, just as the teachers strive to help each student find success. The library media specialist views the entire school in much the same way a teacher sees the classroom. If students in the class fail to achieve, the teacher feels responsible. Likewise, the instructional consultant feels responsible when a teacher in the school is failing to reach potential.

Planning Aids

Planning forms for instructional activities can be found in books and periodicals; two will be mentioned here. The form presented by Jan Buchanan in *Flexible Access Library Media Programs*[3] has the following sections:

- unit title,
- teacher's name,
- group identification,
- scheduled time and place,
- objectives,
- skills,

- media,
- activities,
- end product,
- responsibilities,
- evaluation, and
- comments or suggestions.

In essence, a planning form should provide spaces for telling the what, who, when, and how of the instructional activity. It can also designate which professional (media specialist or teacher) has what responsibilities. A clarifying element is to divide the objectives into two categories, one category for the classroom instructional objective(s) and the other for information or media center objective(s). The following example illustrates these categories:

Instructional objective: The student will be able to discuss three ways that traditions affect culture.

Information objective: Identify and retrieve three sources of information to illustrate traditional costumes from a selected country.

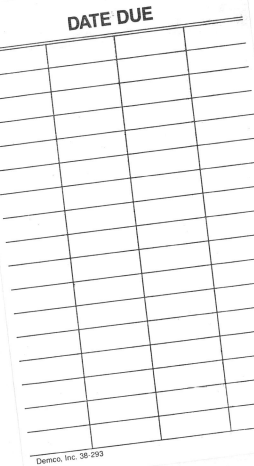

The information objective stated here involves *using* information. Other skill components are finding, locating, organizing, and sharing information.

Advance planning is intended to ensure that instruction and practice in information skills are woven into classroom content. As students learn course content, they also become proficient information users, which should enable them to continue as learners throughout life, long after leaving school. There little doubt that individuals who know how to access and use information ve a distinct advantage over those who do not, both in and out of school.

A second planning form is found in the book by Cleaver and Taylor, *Instructional Consultant Role of the School Library Media Specialist.*[4] Called "Cooperative Planning Guide," this form has space to record the teach- name, date of the unit, and the unit topic. Space below the heading record subtopic, the resources to be used, to indicate who is re- sible for the activity, and to list any equipment needed. The form on was developed and used by this writer. It is a simple way to record objectives, activity, group size, time needed, resources to be used, ethod of evaluation. It can be copied and used as needed or adapted. ee to share the form with colleagues and teachers.

Vhen planning has been completed, the teacher uses the planning ɔ direct students and to gather evaluative data. The library media st uses the form as a reminder of the resources and space that need ailable in the media center at a specified time and for a specified of students.

The planning team reviews planning forms that have been completed over a period of time to determine whether a variety of strategies were used, which strategies seemed to work most effectively, whether an assortment of

Planning Form

Unit Goal

↓

Instructional Objective

↓

Information Objective

↓

Activity

↓

Group Size

↓

Time Needed

↓

Resources

↓

Evaluation

resources were used, how students were grouped for activities, and whether there are apparent gaps in skills developed or content covered.

Focus on Results

Evaluation is an important component that is often missing from library media activities. Yet it is essential that teachers, students, and the media specialist have a clear measure of success. As educators, we know that learners are more likely to learn when the task is carefully spelled out. Whenever students go to the library to complete a task, it is important for the teacher to specify clearly what is expected upon their return. Otherwise, the trip may be seen as busy work with little meaning.

This point is far too important to gloss over; it should be stressed as the focus of learning. *Use of the library should have instructional validity that is apparent to the learner.* The teacher's attitude must convey to the students that the library activity is important. Ultimately, the teacher is the key to whether or not a student is successful in reaching both instructional and information objectives. When a student returns from the library media center, the teacher must be certain to ask for the product, review it within a timely period, and provide feedback to the student. Whether the product was a word definition, or three facts, or a comprehensive report, or a product such as a time line, the end product must be specified and evaluated. Failure to take these important steps soon signals students that they can do whatever they want in the library because they are just there to pass time. Cooperative planning and careful evaluation can ensure their time is not wasted.

A good way for teachers to specify the expected product is to include it on the library media center pass, such as the one provided in Appendix C of this book. To lessen the teachers' paperwork, prepare passes that already include each teacher's name and room number.

People resist forms almost as much as they resist change, but at least in the beginning, there has to be some strategy for planning. At first, you can use planning forms and records to help structure and facilitate planning; later, the same considerations can be noted in a less structured way. The author has found that specialists who use the plan find it takes thirty to forty minutes to complete an activity in the beginning. The time required decreases rapidly as the teachers and media specialist began to speak the same language. When the library media specialist has the necessary background information about the instructional program and if the teacher is clear about instructional intent, an activity can be planned in ten to twelve minutes. Of course, there will have to be a follow-up session to dissect results of the evaluation or end product.

Easing into Planning

Some library media specialists are leery about the planning process because they fear rejection from teachers or they are uncertain about their ability to contribute to the instructional plan. Mostly this is nonsense, because many media specialists are trained and experienced teachers. However, if you are hesitant to jump into the cooperative planning waters, consider a phased-in approach. As you review the four service levels that follow, consider where you currently are and where you want to be.

Level 1   Recommend relevant resources. "Send me everything you have on the Revolutionary War."

Level 2   Recommend resources pertinent to an objective and specific learner need. "Johnny needs additional material to understand the *causes* that led to the Revolutionary War."

Level 3   Assist in structuring the activity. "We need to plan a more active approach for Group 3, perhaps a reenactment of colonists planning the Boston Tea Party."

Level 4   Assist in structuring the unit. "Let's look at our common learning goals for the unit to see where options such as independent study, collaborative groups, and activity centers might fit."

Planning Record

Just as a teacher keeps records of student activities and performance, the library media specialist should record the date and outcome of each planning session. Among other things, this will show whether all teachers are using the library media center's collection.

The library media specialist also needs a record of the activities that are planned, the period of time required, and the number of students who will be involved. Although the teacher will probably determine which students will be involved in which activities, the media specialist needs to know how many, for how long, doing what, and when they are expected to return to class. This is the management role of the media specialist. Below is an example of the type of notes the library media specialist might take during project planning.

Monday, 2/6   Four students from Miss Valentino's class will meet in the media center to identify words the class might not know in the upcoming textbook chapter.

Tuesday, 2/7   Four students will look up definitions in both general and subject dictionaries to define the words identified by the first group.

Wednesday, 2/8   Four more students will locate examples of the words used in sentences in books or articles other than the textbook.

Thursday, 2/9   Four students will look for pictures of the nouns on the list.

Friday, 2/10   Four students will preview videotapes to find illustrations of processes on the list.

As each group returned, the classroom teacher checked the expected product because the following day's work depended on the quality of that day's work. The final performance outcome was a complete illustrated glossary. The media specialist made notes about what occurred while the students were in the media center; the teacher noted classroom performance and learning difficulties. Later, the teacher and the media specialist compared notes.

While this process does increase the paperwork and recordkeeping, it also provides greater direction for the instructional program. Modern management methods emphasize the importance of data gathering for decision making. The data guide the professionals in identifying needed changes and provide a record of what has been accomplished (or at least provide evidence that can be analyzed to see what mistakes were responsible for a lack of accomplishment).

Planning Frequency

How often should library media activities be integrated with classwork? The obvious answer would seem to be constantly, but in reality and in the beginning, try to plan at least one or two activities per unit. If this is done it will be a step forward in most schools. This is not to suggest that twice a unit is a stopping place, for the goal is to have library media resources used routinely each day.

In the beginning, set a goal of planning cooperatively for one media center activity per unit. An average-sized school has thirty-five classrooms. Teaching units last an average of a month to six weeks. This would require planning with thirty-five people for thirty-five activities every four to six weeks. At thirty minutes per planning session, it will require seventeen and a half hours. Fortunately, there are usually days at the beginning and end of the year that are set aside for planning and staff development. Use time during these days for advance planning with teachers. There are also opportunities in many schools for team or grade level planning, which will lessen the hours required. As the planning process becomes more streamlined and past activities are repeated, the planning task seems less onerous.

There must be a commitment of all parties for joint planning to succeed because people can always find an excuse to avoid it or skip it. Once the results show the positive effects, commitment will increase. Before this happens, however, it may be necessary for the library media specialist to remind teachers, perhaps even to implore a few.

Scheduling Library Media Activities

When developing a media center schedule, first record major and school-wide activities for the year. These events include film festivals, book fairs, science fairs, young authors' week, standardized testing, health checks, etc. Next, schedule full class or multiclass activities such as outside speakers, special productions, films, etc. Make schedule notations about classroom topics that require intensive library research or production. Dates on which units are initiated or culminated should also be noted on the media program schedule because of the time needed to supervise students as they select classroom collections, complete glossaries, develop displays, and prepare bulletin boards. Culminating activities are good opportunities for the media specialist to visit classrooms since this allows students and teachers to share their accomplishments. These visits also provide a good opportunity for media specialists to learn more about classroom instruction, to get a better grasp of the topic, and to discern which materials were effective.

Summary

Collaborative planning weaves together classroom content and information skills acquisition. If a library media specialist wants to assist teachers in improving the quality of classroom instruction through planning curriculum-based activities, she or he must be fully informed about the instructional program. This knowledge is gained through reviewing the courses of study, curriculum guides, textbooks, lesson plans, and test data. With this information, a library media specialist is prepared to plan cooperatively with teachers. When teachers become aware the library media specialist has this knowledge, their attitudes about the media center and their perceptions of the librarian's role changes.

It is helpful to use an instructional design framework when teachers and librarians collaborate in developing curriculum-based activities. Considerations involved in using the framework can result in an instructional plan that includes the elements for success: clear purpose, awareness of prior learning and individual learning needs, application of new content, suitable grouping and pacing, targeted materials, and appropriate evaluation. The process proceeds more smoothly when a planning form such as the one presented in this chapter is used. Once a planning form is completed, it is useful to both teachers and the librarian as a reminder of what needs to be prepared and what is to be accomplished.

Notes

1. Michael B. Eisenberg, "Curriculum Mapping and the Implementation of an Elementary School Library Media Skills Curriculum," in *The Emerging School Library Media Program,* ed. Frances Beck McDonald (Englewood, Colo.: Libraries Unlimited, 1988), 228.

2. William E. Hug, *Instructional Design and the Media Program* (Chicago: American Library Association, 1975), 13.

3. Jan Buchanan, *Flexible Access Library Media Programs* (Englewood, Colo.: Libraries Unlimited, 1991), 69.

4. Betty P. Cleaver and William D. Taylor, *The Instructional Consultant Role of the School Library Media Specialist,* School Library Media Programs: Focus on Trends and Issues, no. 9 (Chicago: American Library Association, 1989), 47.

6

Teaching
Information
Skills

A s stated earlier, the best way to teach information skills is by embedding them in, or meshing them with, classroom content. For many years, school librarians tried to teach students about library organization and how to access reference sources with little success, whatever the approach or media they used. Any Education 101 text can explain why they failed—it was because the skills were taught out of context and the learners thought them irrelevant to their needs; that is, the learners were unmotivated and lacked a purpose for learning. Today's approach reverses that situation by instructing at the point of need and planning to ensure that appropriate needs arise.

Information Skills Defined

What are information skills? The 1988 guidelines in *Information Power* labeled them "media skills," while traditional terminology refers to them as "library skills." These skills enable a person to identify needed information, locate it, digest it, and use it. These are the most basic of skills because they are needed every day throughout our lives. An individual faced with a decision asks, "What do I need to know to make this decision?" It may be as simple as knowing what is showing at the movies, or the address of a meeting place, or the calorie content of a particular food. In more important decisions, having timely and appropriate information can truly be the difference between success and failure. Three instructional goals are used to categorize information skills; they call for students to be able

1. to identify and locate needed information,
2. to use information in an efficient and effective manner, and
3. to share information in ways that suit the task and the audience.

These goals have been analyzed into six areas of skill instruction, areas in which objectives often overlap. Nevertheless, these categories, shown below, provide a means of checking and record keeping to ensure that each student becomes knowledgeable and skillful in all areas. They are

1. Location and retrieval skills
2. Equipment operation skills
3. Research skills
4. Thinking skills
5. Presentation skills
6. Production skills

There are no hard and fast rules that stipulate which skills within these six areas are appropriate for a middle school curriculum. In fact, the very nature of a middle school suggests that students will be involved with a broad range of skill development since there will be students below the norm, at the norm, and ahead of the norm—whatever the norm is!

While not a universal list, the objectives in Figure 6.1 are consistent with those addressed in many middle schools. These objectives are listed by grade level and grouped according to the six skill areas. As new formats emerge and information continues to compound, the parameters of these skills change.

The objectives show how various skills are emphasized in different grades. Notice how the beginning verbs change across the grades so students are expected to perform at higher levels, moving from acquiring skills to using them to distinguish and evaluate. In grades five and seven the emphasis is developing research skills, in grade six the emphasis is thinking skill development, and the mass media are emphasized in grade eight.

In most instances, differences in information skill objectives parallel the differences in the content of courses in the middle grades. It should be apparent how skills are introduced, developed, and extended through the grades. Once learned, a skill must be practiced, combined with other skills, and extended. Students develop skills through frequent application. Once concepts or processes have been acquired, students will be able to transfer them from one learning task to a similar one without direct instruction. An example of such transfer would be using the organizational principles of a library catalog to understand the organizational strategy used in a computerized information database.

Although it is a demanding task, the library media specialist should keep records that will show the stage of skill development for each student in the school. Fortunately, a spreadsheet or database computer program makes record keeping much easier today, and the classroom teacher or teaching team may already have the names listed in a computerized format.

FIGURE 6.1 *Sample objectives for grades five through eight*

Grade 5

Area 1   Location and Retrieval Skills
Uses location guides to find information.
Uses book parts to locate information in books.
Uses dictionary key to determine word pronunciation.
Relates information to different newspaper sections.
Uses biographee's name to locate items in browsing.
Uses cross-references to locate additional information.

Area 2   Equipment Operation Skills
Operates a filmstrip projector properly.
Runs instructional software programs on a computer.
Prints score tallies and other information as appropriate.

Area 3   Research Skills
Scans to locate specific information.
Uses globes and atlases for geographical information.
Uses geographical software to locate information.
Writes a paragraph drawing information from two sources.
Takes brief notes.
Develops a sentence outline.
Interviews people to obtain information on a specific topic.
Skims to locate information.

Area 4   Thinking Skills
Uses context to determine word meaning and author's meaning.
Interprets mood of passages or productions.
Distinguishes fact from fiction.
Interprets italics.
Distinguishes biographies from autobiographies.
Interprets information from line and bar graphs.
Draws conclusions from dictated material.

Area 5   Presentation Skills
Reconstructs a story in correct sequence.
Locates places easily on globes.
Employs descriptive words and humor in writing.
Punctuates and capitalizes titles and quotations correctly.
Portrays characters in spoken parts and participates in choral speaking.

Area 6   Production Skills
Develops a simple transparency illustrating one fact.

(continued)

FIGURE 6.1 *Sample objectives for grades five through eight (continued)*

Grade 6

Area 1   **Location and Retrieval Skills**
Locates information in outside-of-school collections.
Reads and follows printed directions.

Area 2   **Equipment Operation Skills**
Develops beginning keyboard skills.
Runs word processing software program on a computer.
Prints documents as needed.
Operates CD-ROM player through computer to access encyclopedia.
Operates videotape player.

Area 3   **Research Skills**
Uses almanacs and disk-based products to locate statistical information.
Uses gazeteers and disk-based products to locate geographical information.
Uses handbooks and special dictionaries to locate quotations.
Uses current events products to locate different perspectives.
Recalls specific points from dictated material.
Develops a simple bibliography of sources.
Surveys factual material before reading.
Recognizes labels, schedules, and signs as information.

Area 4   **Thinking Skills**
Identifies the best word using a thesaurus.
Identifies bias, colloquialisms, and dialects in materials.
Identifies cause and effect in passages and productions.
Adapts stories to new settings, time periods, or endings.
Distinguishes among myths, fables, folktales, and tall tales.
Distinguishes fact from opinion or belief.
Analyzes passages and productions for content and style.
Analyzes nonverbal communication.

Area 5   **Presentation Skills**
Writes simple reports on assigned topics.
Creates original stories.
Develops charts, graphs, and tables to convey information.
Varies language according to purpose.

Area 6   **Production Skills**
Develops a photographic essay.
Develops an overlay transparency illustrating a process.

Grade 7

Area 1 **Location and Retrieval Skills**
Uses book and periodical indices routinely.

Area 2 **Equipment Operation Skills**
Operates a video camera on a stand and handheld.
Uses word processing and database software programs.

Area 3 **Research Skills**
Correlates notes with outlines.
Uses multiple sources and various formats to obtain information.
Compiles facts to support opinion.
Uses biographical sources for information about people.
Uses directories to obtain information about people.
Identifies alternative sources for information.
Cites audiovisual formats in bibliographies.
Edits written work.

Area 4 **Thinking Skills**
Identifies propaganda devices.
Correlates advertising examples with selling strategy.
Distinguishes between fact and imagery.

Area 5 **Presentation Skills**
Conducts group meetings using appropriate rules of order.
Shows respect for presenters and performers.

Area 6 **Production Skills**
Identifies basics of layout in displays, ads, and illustrations.
Develops models as representations of realia and processes.

(continued)

FIGURE 6.1 *Sample objectives for grades five through eight (continued)*

Grade 8

Area 1 **Location and Retrieval Skills**
Continued use of skills acquired in earlier grades.

Area 2 **Equipment Operation Skills**
Uses graphics software and database of varied illustrations.
Uses audiotape recorder in interviewing community members.
Uses videotape recorder in interviewing community members.
Becomes acquainted with online data retrieval.

Area 3 **Research Skills**
Determines word etymologies using appropriate dictionaries.
Uses specialized dictionaries or glossaries to identify terms.
Recognizes and attends to organizational cues from speakers.
Uses career information sources, including those online.
Summarizes passages, productions, and events.

Area 4 **Thinking Skills**
Recognizes elements of various types of literature.
Evaluates materials using established criteria.
Compares claims made by two or more advertisements.
Compares points made by two or more editorials.
Compares points made in two or more interviews.
Compares news broadcasts with documentaries.
Classifies information and labels appropriately.
Interprets symbols and logos.
Recognizes features of various types of literature.
Identifies stereotypes and visual slanting.
Compares persuasion with entertainment.

Area 5 **Presentation Skills**
Introduces speakers providing interesting information.
Understands and uses figurative language.
Compares formal and informal speech.
Varies style according to audience and occasion.
Participates in and contributes to group discussions.
Incorporates current events to enrich presentations.
Engages in informal debate.
Uses audiovisual aids while speaking.

Area 6 **Production Skills**
Develops flowcharts to demonstrate progressions.
Develops newsletters and handouts using appropriate software.

Information Skills and Instructional Objectives

Ironically, teachers and library media specialists believe that teaching objectives and information skill objectives are unrelated but they are often the same. Finding and using information are an integral part of learning any subject. The author often uses a list of objectives that have been drawn from an information skills list, a language-arts course guide, a science guide, and a social studies guide as an exercise to prove this point. Turn to the form on page 68 to see if you can identify the source of each objective and then turn to the answer key in the notes for this chapter to check your decisions. Use the exercise with your faculty to prove the point that information skills are universally relevant.

Two principles become apparent. First, information skills should not be taught in isolation because they have no meaning in that context. They must be applied to be learned. Second, instructional objectives involving content acquisition and information skill development are similar, if not common, for a variety of courses. Believing in these two principles, the teachers and the library media specialist can plan ways for students to learn both course content and the skills needed to find, use, and share information. Students gain both knowledge and the ability to use it. The examples in Figure 6.2 on page 69 illustrate how one instructional activity can result in both content acquisition and information skill development.

Relating Information Skills to Course Content

The planning process involves specifying what is to be learned, analyzing the information involved, identifying where the information can be located, and deciding upon how the content will be delivered, what the student will do, the expected level of performance, and a strategy for evaluating what learning occurred. These decisions result in a matrix explaining who will do what, where, when, and with which resources.

Testing Prerequisite Knowledge

Before the planning team can determine what is to be learned, it must determine what is already known about the topic or skill. Teachers frequently fail to determine what students already know about a topic or skill, or they assume students have knowledge and skills they do not have. It is far more efficient to devise a way to measure what they know and to begin instuction at that point.

A list of objectives that fifth grade students would be expected to know before the beginning of the year should be administered to determine prior knowledge. What are appropriate ways to measure whether or not students have achieved these objectives?

- Recognize that materials are usually organized by subject.
- Use guide letters to locate words in a dictionary or phone book.
- Select appropriate subject headings to retrieve desired information.
- Use information in a catalog entry to determine the most useful item.
- Use classification symbols as a key to subjects.

Instructional Objectives

Where Were They Listed?

Directions: The following instructional objectives were drawn from either a curriculum guide, a state-adopted course of study, or a list of library skills. After each objective, indicate whether you believe the objective was listed under **LS** (library skills), **LA** (language arts), **SC** (science), or **SS** (social studies).

1. Demonstrate proper care of books and other materials. _____

2. Explain symbols on a weather map. _____

3. Identify symbols associated with traditional holidays. _____

4. Determine the author of a newspaper article. _____

5. Use a dictionary to locate synonyms. _____

6. Recognize the use of propaganda. _____

7. Identify an author's purpose. _____

8. Draw conclusions from implicit information. _____

9. Identify patriotic symbols. _____

10. Identify the sentence that best expresses an idea. _____

FIGURE 6.2   *Course objectives*

Social Studies Example

Course objective: Describe the effects of interaction among social, political, economic, and geographical forces on history.

Information objectives: Use encyclopedias and news indexes to identify specific facts and related dates.

Organize information into categories.

Present information in a visual format.

Activity: Have a student group select a method of categorizing information about causes of World War I and World War II and compare those causes with areas of armed conflict today. Students will select and produce a visual product displaying the information found. A second student group will verify the information provided by the first group.

Evaluation: Product is evaluated using a predetermined checklist. A third student group evaluates the product and their scores are combined with the scores determined by the teacher and the library media specialist. Wide discrepancies among scores are discussed and resolved.

Science Example

Course objective: Explain why some animals are endangered and how they can be protected.

Information objectives: Use a biographical dictionary to obtain information about a person.

Become familiar with noted authors and their works.

Relate events in an author's life to his or her writing.

Activity: As a class activity, read aloud or view the videotape of the Newbery Award book *Julie and the Wolves,* by Jean Craighead George. Ask a pair of students to locate information about the author in *More Junior Authors,* another pair to locate information in *Something About the Author,* and a third pair to examine the book cover. These six students will decide how to compare, categorize, and present the information found to the class. Ask each student in the class to write a paragraph explaining why Ms. George wrote the book and post the cards on the "Opinion Board."

Evaluation: Use a predetermined guide to evaluate the relevance and rationale presented by each student.

Math Example

Course objective: Determine decimal equivalents for simple fractions.

Information objective: Interpret Dewey Decimal System symbols to locate materials.

Activity: Have a group of students convert the decimal portion of fifty or more call numbers to fractions and write each conversion on a slip of paper. Drop the pieces in a box and let each student in the class draw out a piece, locate the material, and write the converted Dewey symbol on the back side of the slip. Use the slips as flash cards for students needing remedial assistance so they can test their own responses.

Evaluation: Use a classroom paper-and-pencil test to determine each student's ability to convert fractions to decimal equivalents.

- Recognize cross-references as ways to find additional information.
- Identify a bibliography as a source of additional information.
- Respond to characterizations, plot, and point of view in literary selections.
- Grasp the writer's technique of personification.
- Identify basic elements of who, what, where, when, why, and how in a factual account.
- Distinguish between fact and fantasy.
- Distinguish between fact and fiction.

One way of measuring prior learning is to have a bank of test items. Another way is to set up testing centers with samples of news accounts, bibliographies with related information guides, reports to compare, etc., and associated questions for each. Let students rotate through the centers and record a score for each. Determine which students need remedial work or direct instruction. Then, pull students with common needs from several fifth grade classes and offer the needed instruction.

There will always be some children who do not know basic information skills when they get to the middle school. Therefore, there must be a plan for remediation. Some media specialists use the centers described above, while others use video or computerized instruction. Peer teaching is also a tried and true method of helping youngsters catch up.

Identifying Desired Information

The first step in planning activities that will combine learning information skills and classroom content is to identify the information that will be used in learning course content. Course content is, of course, information. It is difficult to see how any teacher could claim library media will not extend and enhance classroom information. Figure 6.3 reminds you about the many types of information related to content objectives. The second list shows more precisely the relationship between information and course content.

It is important to know what resources are available to provide, extend, or clarify the information needed for each course. Certainly, the library media specialist must know or determine these information sources, but the critical point is for students to know and determine them. When the library media specialist does all the work, he or she also does all the learning. The professionals plan and guide the process; the students should do the work and the learning! Efforts should be made to make certain that every student uses all standard reference sources within a given time period, such as a semester. Ensuring this requires keeping records. The student record card in Appendix C provides one example for recording a student's selection when asked to "Locate three pertinent facts about [an assigned topic], in an encyclopedia, a nonfiction book, or a handbook and cite the source." The record will indicate which students are limited in the resources they identify and use. A planned effort must be made to expand the information repertoire of students.

FIGURE 6.3 *Classroom information needs*

> ## Types of information
>
> Pictures, illustrations, maps, symbols, definitions, synonyms, antonyms, homonyms, pronunciations, foreign words and phrases, interpretations of foreign words and phrases, news accounts, facts, names, biographies, explanations, dates
>
> ## Course-related information needs
>
> Picture of national leader
> Names of endangered animals indigenous to the Southern Hemisphere
> Map symbols
> Causes of most household accidents
> Scientific terminology related to space exploration
> Mayan artifacts
> Map of South Africa
> Quotes from Thomas Jefferson
> Illustrated water cycle
> Animal classifications
> Books featuring physically challenged people
> Examples of Roman and Greek myths
> Pictures of a hacienda, a villa, and a hogan
> News accounts of a recent earthquake

Planning Activities

What will students do with the information? There are numerous strategies and opportunities for practice. In the beginning it may help to have a list of possible activities. A list of verbs in Appendix B suggests a variety of instructional activities to be developed. It is possible to match a variety of activities and products to any instructional or information objective. Care should be taken by the planning team to ensure each student experiences variety of learning activities and uses a variety of resources.

The next task in cooperative planning is to decide which resources will provide students with the information they need. Make certain that students gain experience with all standard reference tools across a period of time, such as a semester. There are numerous ways of bringing this about, because different activities and information tools can be matched with a number of instructional objectives. This does require both planning and record keeping. A suggested performance chart can be found in Appendix C.

Summary

Information skill development is increasingly important because of the wealth of information that exists. Every student needs to be proficient in identifying, finding, using, and sharing information. Developing these skills should be seamless with learning the content of courses in school. When the teachers and the library media specialist plan together, students are able to learn both content and information skills simultaneously. However, it often takes some persuading to convince teachers that the objectives of teaching library or information skills are the same, or similar, to what they are trying to achieve.

Notes

Key to the quiz on instructional objectives (see p. 68).
LA (language arts), **SC** (science), **SS** (social studies), **LS** (library skills)

1. LA	6. LA, SS
2. SC	7. LA
3. SS	8. SS, LA
4. SS	9. SS
5. LA, LS	10. LA

Supporting
Personal
Development

As important as skill development is, nothing contributes more to preadolescent success in the classroom than having a positive self-concept. A concerned and caring media specialist can significantly contribute toward helping students understand and value themselves. There are a number of reasons why a library media specialist is in an advantageous position to help students with their personal development. One is the many opportunities a library media specialist has to work with students individually. Much of the contact between media specialist and student is one-to-one, whether helping find needed information or discussing material a student has read. Most often these moments occur in the media center because it offers an environment apart from the tensions that are often associated with the classroom. Students are often involved in pleasurable activities in the library, activities that allow them to relax and that prompt them to share their thoughts or feelings. This information is a second reason the library media specialist is well situated to contribute to the self-development process.

A third factor is the number of years over which the specialist has contact with students. Teachers have a more in-depth relationship with students for a year, but it is rare for students to maintain regular contact with teachers once the year has ended, even favorite teachers. Usually the relationship with former teachers consists of fond memories and warm greetings. On the other hand, a relationship with the librarian may be less intense, slower developing, but longer lasting. The media center provides an ideal spot for observing student development because it is the only student-centered place where everyone belongs for as long as they are enrolled. Peterson says it best:

> One place in the school belongs to everyone. Only one place is truly a public place. Other places in the school belong to individuals and groups. . . . Entrance into a classroom or office is granted according to reason, but the doors are open into a media center. We walk right in and need not share our reason.[1]

Like the relationship of the coxswain to a rowing team, the job of a library media specialist differs from that of the classroom teacher, but it can contribute just as much to a winning race. Both professionals must be involved in meeting the personal needs of students if the goal is to be reached. The tasks at hand include helping students develop self-esteem and find success, to providing consistent and fair treatment, ensuring successful peer relationships, and helping students find meaning in life. Educators realize that preadolescents are in a developmental period in which they are expected to challenge authority and to explore their own limits. These behaviors are viewed as healthy developmental signs, even though they often frustrate parents and teachers alike.

During preadolescence, a student's feeling of insecurity causes even a small flaw to seem a monumental disaster, a point that was poignantly recalled in a visualized memory by Mary Compton, who is now a middle school authority.

> I saw a tall, gawky, red-headed, freckled-face child/woman. I was already five feet eight inches tall, and I had reached menarche nearly two years earlier. I was beginning to acquire a pimple or two which seemed to appear overnight and I was certain that my skin was the most noticeable part of me.[2]

It is natural for preadolescents to be overly concerned or preoccupied with themselves. This preoccupation causes anything unusual to fill them with feelings of uncertainty. Compton continues recounting her own experiences, saying that during her twelfth year she discovered adult mystery fiction through the writings of Edgar Allan Poe, a find that became a lifetime reading pleasure. Was it the school librarian who was responsible for guiding her to be involved with something outside herself that developed into a favorite pastime? She doesn't say, but it could have been. It could have been if there was a relationship between the two that was based on knowledge that an overly tall-for-her-age girl just might need a place to escape for a while. It could have been if there was a relationship between the two that fostered a perception of the school librarian as a supportive friend and trusted role model. This is the most important way a library media specialist can foster the human development of middle school students.

If library media services are to help students understand themselves and feel good about themselves, then the library media specialist must understand their need to assert their independence, to experiment and sample the real world, to challenge rules and regulations, to disobey in order to gain peer approval, to mimic adult behaviors, and to seek security by group association. Preadolescents sometimes behave erratically and unpredictably as they struggle to find out who they are, form a value system, and develop a sex role identity. When this type of behavior is seen as normal for their age, it causes less consternation and frustration for adults who work with them and for the preadolescents themselves.

Educators know that students' personal needs must be addressed before they can adequately address instructional tasks. Library media specialists help ready students for learning by helping them address their need for peer association and approval. This is done by regularly scheduling sessions in which students can share their thoughts, ideas, wishes, fears, uncertainties, ambitions, and opinions. Group discussions centered on books, developmental concerns, or current issues help students feel part of the crowd and make them aware that others have similar reactions and concerns. When students internalize this, they are more likely to be willing to reach out, to leave the security of the group. It is at this stage that they move from a need for group association to a need for recognition from the group.

> [T]he individual desires a sense of self-esteem within the group. At this point students appear to blossom. Their motivation to succeed grows and they become increasingly concerned with building their own skills. They no longer are just satisfied with belonging to the group; they now desire to derive their self-esteem from that group.[3]

Preadolescents are also helped in their personal development by adults who hold fast to fair rules; this gives them something to test but not to topple. They are very sensitive to different rules being applied to similar situations and they protest loud and long when different disciplinary actions result from the same infraction of rules. It offends their somewhat overly exercised sense of fair play and intensifies their feelings of uncertainty because the situation lacks the stable parameters they need. So the best approach with preadolescents is to have rules and procedures that are established through group participation, with penalties for violations clearly communicated in advance, and for the rules to be consistently enforced by adults. This approach provides stability because students know what to expect; it should be the approach followed in establishing media center policies.

The media specialist helps foster the personal development of preadolescents not only through interaction with individual students in the media center but also by working through three programs that are commonly found in middle schools: guidance services, exploratory classes, and community involvement. To provide a background of information for these special programs, media specialists need to develop two files related to the community. One file should contain names of resource people in the community who are available for school programs and a second file should list agencies that offer assistance to individuals or families in need of social, medical, legal, or financial help. Community resource people are individuals with talents, skills, or experiences they are willing to share with students, primarily in the school setting.

Guidance Programs and Media Services

The need for guidance programs in middle schools is dramatized by two facts:

1. This is the age group most often referred for clinical counseling.[4]
2. Suicide is the second most frequent cause of death among this age group.[5]

As shocking as these facts are, they are better understood when one remembers how many pressures are an unrelenting part of preadolescent existence. These pressures are caused by changing bodies, changing expectations, and changing perceptions. With all the changes that preadolescents face, it is not surprising that the pace of change may be too great for some of them to withstand.

Media service support for the guidance program usually involves service directly to students and indirectly through other staff members. Services to students are provided not only through group activities conducted by the library media specialist in the center, but also through activities that are planned in cooperation with the guidance counselor. Furnishing appropriate materials makes up a significant service related to classroom guidance and the couseling program.

Identifying Materials

School librarians have always wanted to know about students' interests in order to match them with reading and viewing materials. This process goes a step further in middle school practice because the library media specialist works with the guidance counselor to identify books and other materials that correspond with situations faced by students, especially troubled ones. This approach is called *bibliotherapy* and it is a technique many media specialists can use effectively, particularly when they have support from the school counselor. It allows readers to discuss their own problems by addressing the problems faced by characters in a book. Often students are able to say how the character probably feels, yet they might never be able to reveal their own similar feelings. Middle school media specialists are always searching for materials that address the real life concerns of their students. This is just one more reason why they must be alert to the types of problems facing youngsters, such as those listed in Figure 7.1.

This list reflects only some of the stress producers that affect the lives of early adolescents. It does, however, suggest the type of materials that might be useful in the guidance program.

Materials are needed that depict characters who are experiencing situations similar to those faced by students because they can often discuss the problems in the book, yet are unable to discuss personal circumstances. Guidance counselors use these materials both to help students deal with negative aspects of their own lives and to provide vicarious insights into human situations they may never experience. A library media specialist is well trained to find just the right resources.

Locating the right resource is the first step but getting it used is the second. This step requires communicating with the counselors to let them

FIGURE 7.1 *Concerns of preadolescents*

Physical Development Factors
>   Obesity, abnormal height (too tall or short)
>   Early breast development
>   Beginning menstruation
>   Freckles or braces
>   Oversized facial features or physical handicaps

Socioeconomic and Life Event Factors
>   Divorce of parents
>   Grandparents living in the home
>   Death or illness
>   Acceptance and popularity with peers
>   Sexual abuse
>   Drugs and alcohol
>   Threat of terrorism or nuclear war
>   Relations with the opposite sex

Intellectual and Moral Concerns
>   Passing tests and making good grades
>   Honesty and loyalty
>   Career interests
>   Participation in extracurricular activities

know about the materials that are available and being certain the materials are readily accessible. Probably the most direct way to communicate is to place the item in the counselor's hand. However, the next most direct way is probably the one most often used, and that is to provide them with an annotated bibliography that specifies the situation or condition that is dramatized in various materials.

Another avenue of communication that can encourage use of library resources is to plan a joint project with the counselors, such as a book discussion group. Most media specialists know how to stimulate interest in a story line or character. They will rarely ask questions that can be answered by a "yes" or "no" because they know this practice stifles discussion; instead, they ask students to compare one character with another, or to compare how different characters reacted to a similar situation, or to describe the character with whom they identify most. There is an effort to let students express personal views through discussions about characters in a book or in art work based on feelings created by reading novels or listening to music. In jointly planned and presented activities, the media specialist can contribute a knowledge of the literature and the counselor can contribute an in-depth knowledge and awareness of student characteristics.

A media specialist must be careful not to assume a judgmental stance or to give personal opinions when discussing problem-based young adult literature because students need opportunities to hear themselves expressing their own reactions and opinions. The media specialist's role is to provide opportunities and invitations to share. Working closely with the school counselor helps media specialists learn how to be empathetic about students' problems without becoming personally involved in the situation.

Promoting Self-Esteem

Most people like to be recognized and valued so it is not surprising that preadolescents also respond to accolades and attention. Student recognition can be given by a bulletin board display of the pictures, stories, or poems they have developed or by arranging time and space for them to develop a display featuring a hobby or outside-of-school activity.

The media center should regularly feature classroom products or activities. Use the tops of bookcases, bulletin boards, display cases, or develop activity centers for this purpose. Use posters, mobiles, handouts, newsletters, radio broadcasts over the intercom, video productions, slide shows, and media center displays as information modes to let others know about things that are happening across the school program. Ask teachers to let small groups come to the center to develop bulletin boards and displays. Establish a schedule so that each teaching team displays classroom projects at least once each semester. Displaying student work not only makes the media center an interesting, colorful place, it also provides an avenue for building students' self-esteem by showing a regard for their efforts.

One of the best ways to improve self-esteem is to help students achieve in class. Many students fail to achieve their potential because they have poor study skills. Special efforts can be made to help such students learn to organize their studies, to schedule their activities so deadlines are met, and to read material in a manner that promotes comprehension. Appendix C contains forms to use for student assigments and evaluation.

Promoting Socialization and Self-Direction

The socialization process is so important for preadolescents that the media center should be both a learning facility and a meeting place for fraternizing with peers. To promote a relaxed atmosphere, there should be comfortable seating, earphones for listening to music, places for quiet conversations, and challenging, mentally stimulating games to play.

Activities in the library media center should be planned to provide students opportunities to interact. Once a week the Bookbirds meet in the media center. This informal service club is composed of eight girls who love to read. Through a special arrangement with a local bookstore, eight paperback copies of selected titles are purchased so everyone is reading the same thing. Each week the group discusses how they feel about what they have read, conjectures about alternative story lines or character development, and relates the stories to their own lives. The primary purpose is sharing ideas, but an important secondary purpose is establishing the habit of lifetime reading.

A group from a language arts class can come together to make up a story in response to a "story starter" presented by the library media specialist. Once the group has the story line, it can be developed as a video program with members of the group taking the role of various characters. An activity such as this not only engages students and sparks their creativity, it gives them an opportunity to hear one another's ideas. Often real-life elements from the lives of the students involved show up in their stories. This gives a student an opportunity to see how others would respond to the problem facing them without the student having to reveal the problem is real.

Individuals can also be engaged in media center activities that help students get to know each other better. A display case can feature collections owned by students, a "Can You Top This?" display can feature tall tales written by students, a bulletin board can feature baby pictures of students with a related contest to see who can identify all the babies. In an effort to win the contest, students begin to collaborate on whom they recognize.

A student media committee with members selected by their classmates could meet monthly to consider library rules and regulations, to evaluate proposed purchases, and to suggest interesting projects. In this way they are learning a community-service role and establishing a feeling of self-direction.

Serving Students with Special Needs

The media center serves all students; therefore, all students must feel welcome. Special education (mentally or physically challenged) students are particularly vulnerable to feelings of isolation. Handicapped youth are often unable to perform at the pace of other students and may be left out because they cannot keep up. At the other end of the student continuum, gifted students often feel isolated because their performance level exceeds the norm, or their ideas and reactions are more mature. Behavior problems can result when students feel isolated or different, because it is painful not to feel a part of the crowd. The media program can provide structured opportunities for all students to participate in activities that help them feel they belong. Since the media center serves the entire school, students can be grouped across grades or classes, combining students who share common characteristics or interests, regardless of age.

There are many ways the media specialist serves as an ally to guidance counselors in promoting the emotional well-being of middle grade students. Often the counselors are aware of a personal problem facing a student but the student is reluctant to discuss the problem. In confidence, the counselor seeks help from the librarian by asking for stories and novels that involve similar situations. Sometimes the librarian can be a more effective sounding board for the student than the counselor. This situation occurs when students mistakenly perceive counselors as only involved with problem students.

Counselors are often asked for information about colleges and careers. As the school's information specialist, the librarian can be certain the most current sources are available. Using the technology that has become a standard part of the library media center, career and college information can be obtained online, ensuring currency. The media center bulletin board can be a message center for part-time jobs available for after-school work.

Counselors and library media specialists also share a resonsibility for helping students develop good study skills. Working together, these professionals can develop better instructional packages and reach more students. The media center can provide a more relaxed setting for conferences than is possible in the counselor's office. The library conference room is a place where counselors can meet with parent groups. Again, the possibilities are almost limitless. These actions strengthen both programs as the library media center becomes a place to be, not just a place to go.

Exploratory Programs and Media Services

Exploratory courses are a staple feature in a middle school program because they provide opportunities for students to broaden their horizons by being introduced to various skills, interests, and experiences. These courses respond to the students' need to sample a wide range of life's experiences, yet do not require them to maintain longtime interest since most exploratory courses only last four to six weeks. Students select a course topic and once a choice is made, they are required to stick with it until the end of the course, which teaches them to be responsible. They learn that even when a regrettable decision is made, commitments must still be honored.

Exploratory courses are taught by teachers who draw upon their own outside-of-school interests or by community volunteers who are willing to come to the school and share their talents or experiences. Topics vary widely, depending on available instructors. Some familiar topics used in these courses include: Art in the Modern World, Nutrition, Photography, Guitar, Puppets, Grooming, Astronomy, Debate, Math Help, Environmental Action, Knitting, Handwriting, Water Safety, and Cooking.

Identifying Materials

These courses are fertile ground for media-related services because they involve a wide range of presentation modes and topics. In fact, a middle school media specialist could spend full time identifying, locating, retrieving, and adapting information just for these courses. Of course, other program demands prevent that from happening. There are several outside-of-school sources that provide useful materials or ideas for exploratory courses.

Newspapers in Instruction Newspapers are one of the least expensive teaching resources available. They are also a medium on which the middle school language arts curriculum concentrates. These two factors suggest that newspapers are an appropriate format to use in teaching a multitude of topics and skills at the middle school level. Newspapers are particularly suited for an exploratory program because the length of these courses allows only superficial treatment of a subject and newspaper articles give abundant information but require a minimum of reading time. Also, exploratory courses frequently concentrate on current events or issues, and newspapers are the best source for that information. News publications are usually filled with illustrations, graphs, and charts to clarify the text, which is especially useful with young learners who still need concrete examples of information.

The Newspaper in Education Program is particularly useful when developing an exploratory course or single activity. This program is a cooperative effort between schools and newspapers to encourage students to develop lifetime newspaper reading habits. Directed by the American Newspaper Publishers Association Foundation and the Canadian Daily Newspaper Publishers Association, these programs are available in many cities across the United States and Canada. They differ from city to city, depending upon the policies and level of support of the sponsoring newspaper. Typical features include the availability of newspapers in classroom lots for a reduced price and the provision of workshops for teachers. For an extensive bibliography of free and reasonably priced materials related to this program, write: ANPA Foundation, The Newspaper Center, Box 17407, Dulles International Airport, Washington, DC 20041.

A good illustration of newspaper-based instruction was provided by Virginia Riggs, a Texas middle grade English teacher interested in helping disadvantaged students obtain the skills they needed to earn a living. With this goal in mind, she developed an essential skills reading program using the newspaper as the instructional material. She arranged for a classroom set of newspapers to be delivered each day and asked her students to buy a spiral notebook to use as a continuous progress record. First, the purpose of each newspaper section was explained and students were given time to read that section of the paper. In the beginning, the notebook was used to record answers to specific questions, answers that could be found in each day's issue of the newspaper. Every answer had to be written as a complete sentence. Once students mastered the skill of writing a complete sentence, they moved to paragraph construction. Through this instructional approach, students not only improved their skills in reading and writing, they also learned a lot about community affairs and services.[6]

Government Agency Resources   Government agencies are also good sources of information that can be used in exploratory courses. As students mature, their interests expand from their peers to the community and on to world concerns. State and national agencies provide textual and pictorial materials that can be adapted for courses to encourage this transistion. Federally sponsored materials can be identified through an index called the *Monthly Catalog,* which is an index to government publications that can usually be found in large public or academic libraries. Many of the materials listed in this index are inexpensive and they are usually in the public domain, which means the information may be freely duplicated or adapted.

ERIC (Educational Resources Information Clearinghouse) is another government-backed source of information that can be used to find curriculum suggestions. There are two ERIC indexes, one for education periodicals and one for documents that are published in both microform and paper form. *Resources in Education* is the index for the documents, most of which are in the public domain. Each title in this database is identified by an education document (ED) number. Use these numbers to identify the publication wanted. Although publication of this index is supported by the federal government, the materials listed in it have been developed by individuals and by private institutions and agencies as well as by public institutions and agencies.

The following titles from this collection could be used as a basis for planning exploratory courses:

Student Workbooks

The Cemetery: An Outdoor Classroom. Project KARE, ED 142 488

City Street: An Outdoor Classroom. Project KARE, ED 142 489

Curriculum Guides

Graphic Communications. ED 147 461

An Energy Curriculum for the Middle Grades. (World Cultures) ED 187 554

Writing Power. (Functional Writing) ED 197 360

Into Adolescence: Avoiding Drugs. ED 332 067

Mini-Units and Learning Activities

Ride On! (Public Transportation) ED 147 583

Pedal On! (Bicycles) ED 147 591

Environmental Education, Values for the Future: Ecosystems. ED 149 986

People, Parties and Politics. ED 152 603

Around the World.
    Brazil ED 219 976   India ED 219 977
    Japan ED 219 978   Peru ED 219 979

Close Encounters with Everyday Math. ED 233 904

State and Regional Resources Materials produced or published by the state government are usually of interest to middle level students because they contain familiar sites, names, landmarks, or events. Most states have tourist agencies or archives that are rich resources for illustrated brochures, maps, historical documents, and pictures. These materials can be used in either regularly taught social studies units or exploratory courses.

Closely related to the study of a state is the study of the culture in a particular geographic area. One successful curriculum project became a fine arts success through the study of a local area. *Foxfire* resulted from one teacher's effort to find course content that would interest unmotivated students. What he found was the life around the school, for he engaged the students in reading and writing about the culture of the surrounding area.[7] Who would have expected that one teacher's search for interesting course material would one day result in a Broadway production, a television special, and a series of books—but Eliot Wigginton's did! Most people are interested in what others are doing or thinking. Just listen to any casual conversation and it will be evident that discussing others is a favorite topic of conversation for preadolescents. A study of local culture simply puts their natural interest in an instructional framework.

Studying people who live in different areas of a state can provide the basis for creative productions by students. Pictures from a visit to grandparents might be developed into a slide and sound presentation, with the narrative taped on site at the grandparents' home. An illustrated scrapbook can be created from letters written by individuals who describe how they celebrate a favorite holiday. When collecting the letters is combined with an investigation of how the holiday originated, the activity combines sociology and history. This could provide the basis for an excellent exploratory course.

Museums and Galleries As Resources   Many museums, especially those located in metropolitan areas, have education departments or resource centers that furnish materials to schools or provide school tours. The school media center should have a list of such resources, and the description should specify the services or materials they offer and give the name of a contact person.

The St. Louis (Missouri) Art Museum is representative of the services offered by museums today. "ABC" (Art in the Basic Curriculum) is designed to integrate the art collection into classroom content through language arts, social studies, and art courses.[8] Museum personnel join with teachers to provide both museum-based and classroom-based experiences that are tailored to class needs. Projects sponsored by the museum can usually be shared with the total school community. For example, one class in the St. Louis area studied the museum's Northwest Coast Indian art collection and later designed and constructed totem poles, which they displayed in the halls at school. The library media center would also have been a good display site.

The St. Louis museum also provides traveling art exhibits called "Art Access" for students and teachers who are too far away to visit the museum. Atlanta's High Museum of Art offers a program of this type called "Suitcase Exhibits." Similar programs are offered by art and science museums in other cities. Materials furnished by these institutions are usually free or inexpensive to rent. Although using these resources does not usually require a lot of money, it does require time and effort to determine availability and schedule in advance.

Professional Resources   Many media or teaching publications regularly furnish notices about free and inexpensive programs and publications. Some of these magazines are the *School Library Media Quarterly, School Library Journal, Emergency Librarian,* and *American Libraries.* Many of these materials can be used in course work, exploratory courses, or media center activities. An example of this type of material is a booklet, *Study Guide for a Mini-Course on Death,* that was prepared a number of years ago by Lou Willett Stanek for Avon Books. This publication provides teaching tips and study questions for several popular young adult books that include *Go Ask Alice, The Loners,* and *Dreamland Lake.* While these examples may be somewhat dated, similar publications regularly appear.

Other items can be located through news sections of educational journals. One item found several years ago is a copyrighted musical play for middle school students, entitled *Coming of Age,* which is available from the National Association of Secondary School Principals, headquartered in Reston, Virginia. Another interesting product was an illustrated pamphlet entitled *Bridging the Gap: What's Happening Now* by Dr. Robert Hatcher, a medical consultant at the Emory University Family Planning Program in Atlanta. This pamphlet furnishes information about the physical concerns of teenagers. These are only two titles of many that can be discovered by searching through news releases and notices. Usually titles that are exposed in this manner are items that are not distributed through the standard marketplace. Quite often these items are available for only a brief period of time. Their ephemeral nature mandates that searching for new titles continue.

Teaching Exploratory Courses

The library media specialist is always responsible for supervising students who use the media center during exploratory periods, but sometimes the specialist will also instruct an exploratory class. If there is only one person staffing the media center this can be like juggling while dancing. It can be done, although it is much easier when there is a paraprofessional to supervise students while the professional has a class. In a one-person center, media center procedures and policies must be well established so the center continues to operate while the specialist is involved with the exploratory class. Topics a library media specialist might offer as exploratory courses include study skills, award-winning books, female authors, TV production, library service club, developing displays, survey of banned books, or use of biographical reference sources. Sometimes media center time can be scheduled during the exploratory period as a nesting place for students who want some independent reading or thinking time. The school media center should be available for use as the public library is sometimes used, as a sanctuary as well as an information source.

Community Involvement and Media Services

Community involvement is another way in which middle schools can foster the personal development of students. Early adolescents must try out various behaviors in order to determine what fits them, and this means they need exposure to many role models to observe a variety of behaviors. Members of the school faculty serve in this capacity, but they are not enough. The more people who are involved in the school program, the more available role models there are, which is an important reason why students need projects that take them out into the community and activities that bring citizens into the school. Middle school students are also widening their world, changing focus from being family and peer centered to more community and world centered. This too argues for a strong community involvement component in a middle level school program.

A third reason for involving the community in the middle school program revolves around the characteristics of preadolescents. This developmental period can be especially frustrating for adults who come in contact with these students because of their changeable behavior patterns. Frequent communication that helps the general public remember the complexities of the preadolescent age can build tolerance for their sometimes zany actions. Just as citizens seem to approve more highly of schools they know, people tend to be more understanding of youth they know personally. School programs can use involvement in community affairs as a means of developing a friendly relationship.

In fact, community involvement can provide a double benefit for school programs. It helps obtain citizen support for local schools and it can provide a source of volunteers for the school. At a minimum, a strong school and community relationship builds goodwill. The library media specialist can assist with the community involvement program because it requires careful planning, efficient record keeping, and thorough evaluation, just the skills most media specialists have. The media facility can serve as a meeting place, an organizational agency, a materials depository, an office for volunteers, an information conduit, and a museum or concert hall.

Serving Existing
Programs

If the school already has a community volunteer program, the media specialist can operate a clearinghouse for volunteers. This function requires keeping one file for teachers' requests for assistance and a second file for community volunteers. This volunteer file will be separate and different from both the Community Resource File and the Community Services File. The Resource File lists information about community residents who have agreed to share special talents or experiences as part of the instructional program and the Services File lists organizations that furnish social and health services for students and their families. The Community Volunteer File will probably include parents, volunteers from local civic or service organizations, and retired citizens. All three files are needed in every school program and are equally valued, but it is best to keep the lists separate.

Several forms should be developed: (1) an information form for each volunteer that gives name, address, phone number, skills (such as keyboarding ability), schedule availability, and type of service activity preferred; (2) teacher request form that describes their needs and time when help is needed; (3) volunteer assignment and schedule sheet; (4) prewritten notes that can be filled in as to time and assignment, to send as reminders to both teacher and volunteer; (5) weekly schedule forms; and (6) activity summary report forms.

Organizing a
Community Program

The first step in developing a community-based program is deciding the purpose of the program. The next step is planning how the program will operate and who is responsible for implementing it. Planning can be very taxing because it involves many actions which are familiar because they are similar to those taken in program planning and instructional planning. The actions needed are to find out what services are needed in the community, recruit and train volunteers, and schedule them to provide the needed services.

Clearly stated explanations must be given to the community partners about the program's expectations. These parameters should be provided in both verbal and written form. Remember many of these adults will be involved in a new activity, and those who are not parents may never have been in the building. If the program is to succeed, it is important for them to feel as comfortable and self-assured as possible. Complete and clear directions will help accomplish this.

A different type of community involvement project, "Communicate through Literature," has been organized by Pat Scales, the library media specialist at the Greenville (South Carolina) Middle School. The object of this program is to expand parents' knowledge of current young adult literature and to encourage parents to use this literature as a basis for open conversations about teenage problems.[9] Books used in this program are selected by both teenagers and trained project leaders. Selection criteria include: honest characterization, believable plot, and relationship to teenage concerns. The parents read the books, discuss them as a parent group, and then later discuss them with their sons or daughters at home.

This is only one example of how media specialists can involve parents in the school program or in media center activities. This activity involves parents in reviewing and sharing materials, but parents might also enjoy coming together for a work day or evening to help prepare instructional materials for classroom use or to evaluate the effectiveness of a video. Invite parents and others to a "drop-in" equipment operation workshop. Many adults do not know how to operate a slide projector, a microcomputer, or a video recorder and they might welcome an opportunity to be instructed by a student media aide. It is not as important what community members do as it is to involve them in school affairs.

Serving As an Arts Center

The community can be brought into the school through the media center when it is used as a showcase for their talent. Most media centers have flexible schedules and open spaces that make it possible to accommodate a craft demonstration, display art works, or present a piano recital or poetry reading. This approach can convert the school media center into an art museum or concert hall for the benefit of students and staff. There is mutual benefit for school and town—the school provides good exposure for amateur artists and students become more knowledgeable about the creative arts.

Taking Students into the Community

Community and school cooperative programs also provide opportunities for students to be involved in civic or charitable activities. The Harper's Choice Middle School in Columbia, Maryland, provides opportunities for students to work in community service jobs during the exploratory period.

For example, students can apply for jobs in which they assist handicapped persons at a nearby facility. The students then work at this job during their exploratory class period. As they help others with therapy, eating, or moving about, the students learn more about themselves. It is easy to see how such experiences provide assurance and sense of well-being for the middle school students who participate in them.

Middle school students have many skills and talents to share and sharing helps develop self-concept, a sense of compassion, and feelings of self-worth. Schools should be alert to possibilities to connect interested students with community services, such as reading to blind individuals, teaching computer operation to senior citizens, delivering food to housebound individuals, or helping with a mailing for the community chest. Properly organized, and with district-level support, students can become involved in activities that let them share their own resources while gaining experience in working with others.

Media specialists can help organize these activities by contacting community agencies to determine areas of service where help is needed and discussing these with the media committee to identify the most appropriate ones. Even when a school's location restricts student access to other agencies or institutions, students can be involved in community service projects. Many school communities collect food for distribution during holidays, write cards to service personnel or shut-ins, develop art work or puppets for hospitalized children, and hold story hours for young children at the public library. There are so many needs to be filled and middle school students have such a keen sense of compassion that it seems particularly appropriate to involve them in service activities. For many youngsters, it may be the beginning of a lifetime habit of helping others.

Communicating with the Community

There are at least two ways in which the media specialist can serve a school community by acting as a communications agent. Let parents and other interested individuals know what is being accomplished in the school program by becoming the school's official hornblower. Since the media program operates at the center of the school program, no one is in a better position to know about special projects and activities that are taking place in classrooms.

Develop a newsletter with one of the many simple-to-operate computer programs that are now available or organize a small student group to prepare and produce a school-to-community information sheet. This activity can be good training for future editors, copywriters, and artists. It might also be valuable as an exploratory course taught within the media center. In addition, the media specialist can also routinely prepare news releases for the local paper, acting in conjunction with the school administration.

A second communication service is providing information for parents. Such information might describe available health services, alert parents to the observable characteristics of drug use, suggest considerations to use in developing a home study area, or announce upcoming events. All these activities are constant with the library media specialist's role as provider of materials and information for the school community.

Summary

A concerned and caring media specialist can significantly contribute toward helping students understand and value themselves. The media center schedule makes it possible for a library media specialist to interact with small groups and individuals. The facility provides a more relaxed atmosphere than an office or classroom. It is one place in the school where everyone belongs.

Belonging is important to everyone, but it is extremely important to preadolescents. They are perplexed by changing bodies and uncertain about changing feelings. Any place that can help them feel good about their abilities, can whet their interests, and can help them interact with others in positive ways will be an important place in their world. This is the challenge for library media specialists in all schools, but especially in middle schools. A library media specialist must be aware of the concerns of preadolescents and must look for ways to address those concerns. Myriad opportunities exist to promote self-direction and self-esteem, opportunities that range from book clubs to community service projects.

Notes

1. Ralph L. Peterson, *A Place for Caring and Celebration: The School Media Center* (Chicago: American Library Association, 1979).

2. Mary Compton, "The Twelve-Year-Old Within," in the President's Page column, *Middle School Journal* 8 (November 1981): 24–25.

3. John P. Deibert and Kevin J. Walsh, "Maslow and Team Organization," *The Clearing House* 55 (December 1981): 169–70.

4. Stanley J. Herman, "Middle School Interdisciplinary Teaming and Reinforcement Systems," *Middle School Journal* 5 (Fall 1974): 33–36.

5. Conrad F. Toepfer, Jr., "No Greater Potential: The Emerging Adolescent Learner," *Middle School Journal* 4 (Spring 1973): 3–6.

6. Virginia Riggs, *Johnny Can Read!* Reprint of speech delivered at the 1968 University of Iowa Newspaper in the Classroom Workshop. American Newspaper Publishers Association Foundation (n.p., n.d).

7. Eliott Wigginton, *Foxfire* (Garden City, N.Y.: Doubleday, 1972).

8. Hedy Ehrlich, "Saint Louis Art Museum, Rich in Tradition and Education Programs," *Arts and Activities* (September 1982): 30–33.

9. Pat R. Scales, *Communicate through Literature: Introducing Parents to the Books Their Teens Are Reading and Enjoying* (New York: Pacer Books, 1984).

Evaluating a Curriculum-Based Program

P eople often confuse evaluation and assessment. Perhaps it is because similar techniques are used in both procedures although their purpose is different. Both procedures should instigate action. While neither procedure is essential for program delivery, both are important in gaining program effectiveness. These procedures should not be undertaken just to satisfy some administrator's request or to create an impression of good management; instead, they need to be done because the information they provide is the foundation for a good program. Good programs do not come from intuition, but from informed opinion. Assessment and evaluation provide informed opinion.

Assessment asks, "where are we in relation to where we should be?" Assessment is the same as formative evaluation. It shows what is lacking by comparing what is desired to what exists. For example, if a goal is to implement a curriculum-based program during the school year, and yet there is no evidence of planning between the library media specialist and the teachers by the beginning of the calendar year, there is an obvious need to be addressed. A plan must be devised to initiate planning sessions. Suppose information gathering, probably by reviewing the media specialist's calendar, shows that planning is occurring with sixth grade teaching teams but not with other grade level teams. Adjustments must be made, and success can still be achieved. Assessment is generally more informal, ongoing, and more frequent.

Evaluation, on the other hand, takes a backward glance to answer the question, "How well did we do what we set out to do?" Evaluation is tied to stated goals and objectives. The salesman's goal is to sell 50,000 units this year, but the final sales report shows he sold only 25,000, reaching only 50 percent of his quota. On the surface it would seem the salesman was unsuccessful. However, this trite example brings notice to several points related to evaluation. To be a valid measure, evaluation must measure a reasonable expectation. If the goal or objective is not achievable, the evaluation strategy is useless. Perhaps only 50,000 units were purchased worldwide! Evaluation data must be captured in a dependable manner. Perhaps the actual sales were 45,000 units but the method used to gather the information was a casual phone sample instead of an actual order count. The third point is that evaluation requires careful analysis and reporting if it is to be useful in revising future plans. Suppose the first two digits in the units sold column of the report had been reversed—the salesman's performance would be judged quite differently. Similar consideration should be given to program evaluation.

Although the purpose for the two procedures is different, similar techniques are used in gathering data. Questionnaires are popular devices because they are viewed as relatively easy to construct and summarize. Again, it is important to carefully consider all aspects of any questionnaire. Does the questionnaire elicit responses that reflect program objectives? If not, the information may be useless. Is the questionnaire directed to people who have the information? A good teacher questionnaire and a good parent questionnaire will be different because the perspectives of the respondents are different. Third, the type of response should be appropriate. Questions where respondents must only check a response or circle a number are more likely to be completed by busy people. However, open-ended questions usually result in more information. Other popular evaluation techniques are rating scales, checklists, and interviews.

More important than deciding what type of evaluation to use is to spend time thinking about the type of information desired. Too often evaluation forms are prepared as a way of gathering support for something the library media specialist wants to do, and the results are manipulated so a need is documented or a success is claimed. These "feel-good" questionnaires or rating scales may give the library media specialist evidence of having done a good job, but they do little to provide the information needed to determine if the program services and activities are adequately supporting school goals. Effective evaluation is tied to goals and objectives. If the library media program is to further school goals, then the evaluation strategy should be planned to gather information related to those goals.

In past years, realistic and goal-driven evaluation has been rare in school libraries. Too often a library media specialist maintained there was value in having a library program because she or he just knew intuitively that this was true. Yet in these days of tightening budgets and competing priorities, more accountability is required. It may be nice to have a school library, but does having one ensure that students learn more? This is the bottom line for school libraries. Just as in business, we need to remember the bottom line for that is what determines success.

Assessment and evaluation need to be comprehensive in terms of the program areas and populations tested. For example, all facets of the school community should be measured. An evaluation project that fails to measure student or parent perceptions may miss revealing data. When the library media specialist is uncertain about the effectiveness of some program element, it would be dishonest and short-sighted not to measure it. Not wanting to hear bad news is little reason to short circuit the evaluation process.

While it is amazing that past library media publications have failed to address program assessment and evaluation, the practice is changing. A book by Gustafson and Smith, *Research for School Library Media Specialists,* provides direction in the use of research techniques, with numerous examples drawn from the field of school library media.[1] Morris in *Administering the School Library Media Center* includes a number of forms that can be used as is or adapted for program evaluation.[2] In her revision of the popular Spirt and Gillespie administration text, evaluation forms begin with self-evaluation of the media professional, which seems an appropriate starting point. Both the Morris book and this book contain excerpts from a program evaluation questionnaire used by the Madison, Wisconsin, Public Schools.

This program planning guide includes a number of evaluation forms that can be used or modified as needed. The first four forms are to be filled out by the media specialist. They are used to determine how well the services and activities of the media program have contributed to fostering school goals and objectives, and to determine if the time spent was consistent with the priorities established by the library media committee. These four forms are Contributions to School Goals, Contributions to the Instructional Program, Time Accountability Form, and Time Summary Sheet. Following the forms to be completed by the library media specialist is one borrowed from the media specialists in Madison, Wisconsin. This form focuses on the goals and objectives of the library media program and it should be administered to teachers, administrators, and parents. Naturally, the items should be changed to reflect actual goals and objectives of your program. Next are a skill evaluation form to be completed by the media center staff and teachers and a self-evaluation form for the media specialist to complete. The latter is titled Professional Improvement and Practices Checklist. Last is a questionnaire developed as a way for the principal to test the degree to which suggestions in this book are implemented in his or her school. Using information gathered from these or similar forms, a library media specialist should be armed with information that will make it possible to adjust the program so it is more effective next year.

Notes

1. Kent L. Gustafson and Jane Bandy Smith, *Research for School Library Media Specialists* (Norwood, N.J.: Ablex, 1994).

2. Betty J. Morris, with John T. Gillespie and Diana L. Spirt, *Administering the School Library Media Center,* 3rd ed. (New Providence, N.J.: Bowker, 1992), 499–529.

I. Contribution to School Goals

Directions: List your school's goals. Next, specify the library media activities conducted during the year that related to each school goal. Information about library media activities can be drawn from schedules, time management forms, and sign-up sheets. Determine how much time was expended preparing and providing the activity and indicate how many individuals were served. Use the amount of space needed, not just what is shown.

To foster human and skill development of each student, responding to the great variations in physical, mental, intellectual, and social development.

Activity	Time	Number of Participants

To establish school conduct based on rules that are cooperatively derived, consistently and fairly applied.

Activity	Time	Number of Participants

To provide opportunities for adolescents to share ideas with peers and adults in order to share their experiences, try out their thoughts, and refine their ideas.

Activity	Time	Number of Participants

To provide students with opportunities to explore a variety of ideas, topics, vocations, experiences, and activities.

Activity	Time	Number of Participants

To offer opportunities for community involvement and understanding of civic issues. To develop/reinforce good citizenship practices.

Activity	Time	Number of Participants

II. Contributions to the Instructional Program

Directions: See Section I for recording process. This evaluation seeks to determine how classroom instruction was strengthened because teachers were provided with access to relevant supplementary materials and information.

Resources were supplied by securing nonschool-owned resources, providing original productions, or adapting materials owned by the school to better suit current instructional needs.

Activity	Time	Number of Participants

Teachers were provided appropriate in-service opportunities to help them continue to develop their professional skills.

Activity	Time	Number of Participants

Teachers were supported through cooperative planning between teachers and media specialists to address instructional problems and to integrate information-use skills in classroom course work.

Activity	Time	Number of Participants

III. Time Accountability Form

Directions: Compile the time recorded for activities in Section I and Section II to show how much time each month was spent in service to students and staff. Analyze the amount of time spent each month in the three major areas of responsibility: (1) administration, (2) instruction, and (3) consultation. Do time expenditures reflect program priorities? Is too much time spent in one area to the detriment of the other two?

	Administration	Instruction	Consultation
September	_____	_____	_____
October	_____	_____	_____
November	_____	_____	_____
December	_____	_____	_____
January	_____	_____	_____
February	_____	_____	_____
March	_____	_____	_____
April	_____	_____	_____
May	_____	_____	_____
TOTAL	_____	_____	_____

IV. Time Summary Sheet

Directions: Compute the number of hours spent in activities to support school goals.

Activities for students   _____

Activities for staff   _____

Total activity hours   _____

Directions: Compute hours actually spent in each of the three service areas; then compute percentage of time spent in each area.

Service Area	Hours	Percent of total time
Administration	_____	_____
Instruction	_____	_____
Consultation	_____	_____
Total hours	_____	_____ 100% _____

Directions: Compare the percentage of time actually spent with time priorities established by the library media committee.

	Actual time spent	Priority allocations
Administration	_____	_____
Instruction	_____	_____
Consultation	_____	_____

Response to Library Media Program Goals and Objectives

Directions: The library media center goals are shown below. Objectives for reaching each goal are shown below each goal. These 12 goals and 28 objectives were identified by the Library Media Committee. Please help evaluate how effective the library media staff has been in reaching stated outcomes. Circle the number that indicates the extent to which the library media program goals and objectives have been met.

NK = not known, not offered; 1 = unsatisfactory; 5 = outstanding

1. To cooperatively and systematically plan the library media program, assuring input from students, parents, and staff.

   A library committee that consists of representatives from the school community recommends policies and acquisitions.

   NK   1   2   3   4   5

   The library media program is annually reviewed and a written report indicates the effectiveness of the program in reaching stated goals.

   NK   1   2   3   4   5

2. To consult with individual teachers in designing learning activities and in evaluating learning.

   Teachers are helped to identify, design, produce, or modify instructional materials and strategies.

   NK   1   2   3   4   5

   Teachers are helped to identify and acquire resources needed for professional growth.

   NK   1   2   3   4   5

   Teachers, especially new personnel, are assisted in solving problems related to instruction or classroom management.

   NK   1   2   3   4   5

$\rightarrow$

3. To provide assistance in the identification, location, and use of information, which includes providing direct answers when appropriate.

Up-to-date reference materials are available or information from outside-of-school collections is obtained.

NK   1   2   3   4   5

Bibliographies relevant to the curriculum are provided.

NK   1   2   3   4   5

Adequate and appropriate information resources are available for students with special needs.

NK   1   2   3   4   5

Relevant, pertinent materials are routed to students and staff.

NK   1   2   3   4   5

Appropriate literature is integrated to stimulate classroom activities.

NK   1   2   3   4   5

Teachers are recommended materials that encourage students to view, listen, or read.

NK   1   2   3   4   5

4. To provide a full-range, integrated, media skill instructional program that is cooperatively planned with teachers.

Library media specialist and teachers jointly plan, implement, and evaluate media skill instruction to be appropriate with classroom content.

NK   1   2   3   4   5

5. To provide an opportunity for students to use media for information and recreation in order to foster development of a lasting appreciation for the communication arts.

Library media specialists help individual students select materials that are appropriate with personal interests and needs.

NK   1   2   3   4   5

$\rightarrow$

Library media specialists help parents understand features of school-owned materials and offer guidance in choosing materials for home use.

NK   1   2   3   4   5

6. To provide an environment that contributes to the enhancement of positive student self-concepts and takes into account their individual differences.

Displays and bulletin boards reflect student work and current topics of interest.

NK   1   2   3   4   5

Varied learning styles are accommodated by ready access to multiple formats.

NK   1   2   3   4   5

7. To provide efficient access to varied and well-maintained collections of learning resources that supplement the curriculum and meet student's personal/educational needs.

Materials are organized in a way that encourages use and facilitates easy retrieval.

NK   1   2   3   4   5

Materials reflect the national diversity and contributions of all population segments.

NK   1   2   3   4   5

Technical assistance, facilities, and supplies are available for staff and students who need to produce materials.

NK   1   2   3   4   5

8. To provide a wide variety of resources and information through networking and sharing with other institutions and organizations.

Students and teachers are informed about information or materials that are available from outside-of-school sources.

NK   1   2   3   4   5

9. To provide guidance for students, teachers, and administrators in the ethical use of information, which includes furnishing copyright information and privacy of records.

Media specialists regularly inform the school community about copyright law interpretations and the possible results of noncompliance.

NK   1   2   3   4   5

→

10. To provide equipment, in good repair, for students and staff to use.

Equipment is inventoried, maintained, and circulated by the media staff. (administration)

NK   1   2   3   4   5

Small pieces of equipment are available for overnight circulation to students and staff. (administration)

NK   1   2   3   4   5

11. To provide media facilities that encourage use and accommodate easy access.

Library media center is accessible every day school is in session.

NK   1   2   3   4   5

Library media center is open before and after the regular school day.

NK   1   2   3   4   5

Flexible scheduling accommodates classroom needs and simple sign-up system assures ready access.

NK   1   2   3   4   5

12. To provide information to the community about media center activities and resources and to incorporate community resources into the school program.

Parents are informed and involved in the library media program.

NK   1   2   3   4   5

Students are made aware of community activities and resources through activities in the library media center.

NK   1   2   3   4   5

Goals and objectives from Madison (Wis.) Public Schools are used with their permission.

Information Skill Instruction

Directions: Indicate the degree of implementation you believe exists.

1 = negligible implementation;   5 = well implemented

1. Instructional objectives for information skills are well defined and clearly communicated to teachers.

    1   2   3   4   5

2. An established teaching plan ensures that skills are integrated with classroom work.

    1   2   3   4   5

3. Coordination between teachers and media personnel ensures student development.

    1   2   3   4   5

4. Materials and strategies are prepared for teaching each skill.

    1   2   3   4   5

5. Techniques and materials are varied to accommodate differing student abilities.

    1   2   3   4   5

6. Students are given frequent opportunities to practice information skills.

    1   2   3   4   5

7. Valid evaluative techniques are used to measure instructional objectives.

    1   2   3   4   5

8. All teachers are thoroughly informed about library arrangement, available reference sources, and operation of audiovisual equipment.

    1   2   3   4   5

9. There are adequate opportunities for new students to become oriented and informed about library media opportunities.

    1   2   3   4   5

Professional Improvement and Practices Checklist

Directions: Check all the strategies that have been employed during the past year to improve the skills and knowledge of the library media specialist(s).

_____ Attended workshops and courses for professional development.

_____ Read professional journals and books.

_____ Discussed current curriculum-related topics with knowledgeable persons.

_____ Introduced new equipment/technology/material formats into the instructional program.

_____ Made the faculty aware of current events related to the curriculum or for general professional enrichment.

_____ Attended parent association meetings.

_____ Voluntarily participated in systemwide training programs.

_____ Visited exemplary library media programs in other schools.

_____ Reviewed standards and guidelines for library media programs.

_____ Reviewed schoolwide curriculum, textbooks, and teaching plans.

_____ Reviewed standardized test objectives.

_____ Participated in professional organizations.

_____ Evidenced knowledge of district policies and procedures.

_____ Evidenced interest in wanting to learn and seeking new ideas.

_____ Visited other community institutions to identify materials and human resources.

_____ Read news accounts on a regular basis.

_____ Prepared a plan for professional improvement.

Note: Results of this assessment and the professional improvement plan for the coming year should be shared with the administration during the year-end conference.

Principal's Questionnaire

1. Does your school have written goals?

   Yes _____ No _____ Uncertain _____

   If there are written goals, are they used in specifying priorities for the library media program?

   Yes _____ Occasionally _____ Rarely _____ No _____

   Rank order the following library media services according to the needs of your school's program (number 1–10 with number one being the most important).

   Information referral _____

   Production of materials for instruction _____

   Creative hands-on activities _____

   Information skills instruction _____

   Research guidance _____

   Collection development _____

   Literature enrichment _____

   Library media center management _____

   Reading guidance _____

   Reading motivation _____

2. Do the teachers and the library media specialist rank these functions in the same way?

   Yes _____ No _____ Haven't asked _____

3. In your opinion, does the school library media specialist know what content is included in each subject for each grade of the school?

   Yes _____ No _____ Uncertain _____

→

4. Has the library media specialist discussed plans with you for the library program?

Yes _____ No _____

Has the library media specialist shown you the results of last year's program?

Yes _____ No _____

5. From a social studies textbook currently in use in the school, select a statistic or fact. Look in the library media center's reference section to verify the accuracy of that fact.

Do you know where the reference materials are located?

Yes _____ No _____

Are you aware of reference materials that will probably contain the information needed to check the textbook content?

Yes _____ No _____

Do you know the arrangement of the reference source so it can be used quickly to check the statistic or fact?

Yes _____ No _____

What was the publication date for the reference source you used (this date is usually printed on the title page or the back of the title page)?

_____

Is the publication date within the last ten years?

Yes _____ No _____

6. To accomplish the tasks specified in #5, would your first inclination be to ask the library media specialist to assist you?

Yes _____ No _____

In your opinion, is the library media specialist prepared to help you?

Yes _____ No _____

→

In your opinion, is the library media specialist interested in helping you?

Yes _____ No _____

In your opinion, if a teacher in the school was asked these three questions, would he or she answer in the same way?

Yes _____ No _____ Uncertain _____

7. Other than book check-out, identify two activities in which students have been engaged in the library media center in the past week.

8. Were each of these activities planned jointly by the library media specialist and a teacher?

Yes _____ No _____ One was _____ Uncertain _____

9. When does collaborative planning take place in your school?

10. Compare the media center to your favorite grocery store.

Is it as neat and clean?

Yes _____ No _____

Is it as well stocked?

Yes _____ No _____

Do signs direct you to the things you need?

Yes _____ No _____

Program
Planning Aids
and Examples

*Materials in this appendix are for library media specialists
to use or adapt in implementing a curriculum-based program.*

Philosophy, Goal, and Objectives

These examples were developed by the parents and staff of
Wilkerson Middle School in Birmingham, Alabama. They can be
used by a faculty or library media committee to initiate a discussion
about the purpose of the school library.

Process for Establishing a Library Media Committee

Borrowed from the Georgia Department of Education, a ten-step
process to use in identifying and organizing a library media
committee.

Functions of a Library Media Committee

A list to use in selling formation of the committee to the principal
and in communicating with prospective or current members
regarding tasks to be accomplished.

Classroom Indicators of Library Media Use

A checklist for the library media specialist and principal to use in
determining the relationship between the school library and the
classrooms.

Teacher Alert: Instructional Support Services from the Media Center

This sheet can be used by the principal and library media specialist as an evaluation checklist or it can be a flyer to distribute to the faculty and parents.

Reminders for Today

Borrowed with permission from the DeKalb County (Georgia) School System, this form is prepared at the end of each day as a "to do" list for the following day. As each item is completed, the media specialist checks it off, and at the end of the day determines the rank of the things completed. Rank may refer to priorities or it may indicate (1) important and essential, (2) important but not essential, (3) essential but not important, (4) not essential and not important. Helps in managing time more effectively.

Philosophy of the School Library

We believe that the school library exists for the use of the students in order to provide for their personal intellectual growth and to promote an interest in and an appreciation of the values of human achievement represented in the library's collection of material.

We believe in the free access of all students to the library facilities. We believe that these facilities should be structured to permit the greatest use by the greatest number of students. We believe that aid should be available to all students, and students should be taught to gain self-sufficiency in the use of library facilities.

Goal

To facilitate the use of library services at Wilkerson Middle School.

Objectives

1. The library will be the center of independent study and group work for all students.

2. Individually scheduled work in the common curriculum, as well as on individual projects, will be a central part of the students' education.

Used with permission from Eugenia J. Harris, Library Media Specialist, and Anita Skipwith, Principal, Wilkerson Middle School, Birmingham, Alabama.

Process for Establishing a Library Media Committee

Step 1   In written form, explain the purpose for a media committee and the responsibilities of committee members. Request an opportunity to discuss the committee with the Principal.

Step 2   Ask the Principal to appoint committee members. Be prepared to suggest names of teachers to represent each constituency within the school (by grade level, subject area, etc.). Although you may wish to begin the committee with teachers who are responsive to media services, it is important for future success to include those teachers who rarely use the media center.

Step 3   Have information about the committee in writing so the Principal can hand it to each teacher that is invited to serve on the committee. Specify how often the committee will meet and how long each meeting is expected to last. Explain that reconsideration challenges will require unscheduled meetings, but that these meetings should not occur often.

Step 4   Once the Principal has appointed or invited teachers to participate, go in person to see each one in order to thank them and to answer any questions they have.

Step 5   Schedule the first committee meeting within six weeks. Provide committee members with at least one month's advance notice in writing.

Step 6   Remind committee members the week prior to the meeting by furnishing them with an agenda and any background information that is needed.

Step 7   Arrange to have the committee meet in the office of the library media center or in the workroom, if possible. This arrangement will allow the center to be used by students and staff as needed, yet it will provide an appropriate setting for the committee meeting. It would be nice to have some light refreshments available.

Step 8   Have all materials arranged on the meeting table—note paper and pencils, plus any information that has not been furnished before the meeting. It is also wise to have extra copies of previously furnished material because someone will forget to bring their copy to the meeting.

Step 9   Begin the meeting promptly. Be certain everyone knows the names of all committee members. This can be accomplished by a list for each member, signs on the table, or name tags.

Step 10   Follow the established agenda. Refer other issues to future meetings. Ask one person to act as a recording secretary. Use their notes to develop written minutes of each meeting. Distribute a copy of each meeting's minutes to each committee member and to the Principal. Keep one copy in a file folder as documentation of topics and decisions.

Created for the Georgia Department of Education, Instructional Media Division, Atlanta, Georgia.

Functions of a Library Media Committee

Establish long-range and short-range goals for the library media program.

Set program priorities and recommend services and activities.

Recommend policies for library media center operation.

Inform the library media specialist about service or collection problems.

Recommend areas or topics for purchases.

Serve as a liaison with faculty and parents regarding library media center operation, services, and collection.

Advise others about copyright regulations.

Campaign for support for the library media program.

Recommend selection and utilization policy revision.

Consider requests from others to withdraw material from the collection.

Help evaluate the library media program.

Classroom Indicators of Library Media Use

1. Audiovisual equipment is being used.

   ☐ Equipment is in use or appears to have been used (dust free, uncovered).

   ☐ Teaching plan refers to or implies equipment use.

2. Library books are included in the classroom reading area.

   ☐ There is a variety of topics and reading levels.

   ☐ Books are apparent on tops of student desks.

3. Teachers are using visuals and realia routinely.

   ☐ Lesson plans include references to this material.

   ☐ Teachers can operate equipment effortlessly.

   ☐ Viewing and listening centers have been established.

4. In answering the question, "Why do your students go to the library media center?" teachers respond with specific tasks.

5. Teachers are seen using library resources and trade books for personal enrichment and pleasure.

6. Teachers are conversant about instructional resources that are available from collections outside the school.

Teacher Alert
Instructional Support Services from the Media Center

1. Recommending media for specific purposes;

2. Evaluating the effectiveness of various formats;

3. Reinforcing students' skill acquisition;

4. Identifying examples in literature related to classroom exercises or content;

5. Providing professional information to assist teachers in improving teaching skills;

6. Providing course-related information to help teachers remain up-to-date;

7. Providing in-service programs in equipment utilization;

8. Relating textbook content to information in reference books and outside information sources;

9. Recommending supplementary materials for use in classroom activities;

10. Using the instructional development process in ongoing planning with teachers;

11. Altering or producing materials when needed;

12. Offering staff development programs to promote better utilization of materials;

13. Informing teachers about copyright provisions and decisions;

14. Guiding students to materials that extend or enrich classroom learning;

15. Infusing media skills into course work so that students have the skills they need to effectively acquire and use information;

16. Providing instructional resources cited in textbooks;

17. Maintaining and circulating equipment for available materials;

18. Correlating library books with classroom topics to encourage outside reading;

19. Securing media for classroom use that is not available in the school collection.

REMINDERS
FOR TODAY . . .

"Media Specialists Make a Difference in *A Place Called School*"

Today's Date _____

Task	Rank
1.	
2.	
3.	
4.	
5.	
6.	
7.	
8.	
9.	
10.	
11.	
12.	

Used with permission from Frank Charles Winstead, Director of Media Services, DeKalb County Schools, Decatur, Georgia.

A·P·P·E·N·D·I·X

Instructional
Planning Aids
and Examples

*Materials in this appendix are for library media specialists to use or
adapt in implementing a curriculum-based program.*

Questions to Determine Instructional Intent of Teachers

A short questionnaire to use in determining what a teacher has in
mind before collaborative planning is undertaken.

Checklist of Lesson Plans

A form for recording lesson plans as they are collected from teachers.

Textbook Survey Record Form

A form for making notes as each textbook is reviewed.

Cooperative Planning Guide

Flow chart for the library media specialist to use in instructional
planning with teachers.

Model for Collaborative Planning

A flowchart of things a library media specialist and teacher will do
together as each plan for a group activity is developed and
implemented.

Correlating Library Resources with the Curriculum

Steps to follow in matching available resources with what is being taught. Materials needed for each subject are the curriculum outline and adopted textbook.

Types of Information

A checklist to remind teachers and library media specialist of the many types of information that should be employed as learning tasks are planned.

Verbs Describing Learning Tasks

A checklist to remind teachers and library media specialists to vary the level of learning tasks so students develop higher-order thinking skills.

Sixth Grade Examples of Collaborative Planning

Sample activity plans addressing both content objectives and library media objectives across the curriculum.

Eighth Grade Example of Contract Unit

Used with permission, an example of a contract unit. Students elect the number of activities to complete and select those of greatest interest.

Fifth Grade Information Skills Evaluation

Example of a pretest for entering fifth graders to place them on a skills development continuum. Answers to the test items are given in parentheses.

Key Words to Use in Evaluation

A list of various approaches to use when planning formative and summative evaluation.

Questions to Determine Instructional Intent of Teachers

1. What are your objectives for this unit?

2. Beyond the textbook, what resources will you use?

3. Do you use a work or works of fiction when teaching this topic?

4. How do you think students can be engaged in finding information?

5. What is the best number of students to engage in an activity?

6. How much time is optimal for a group activity?

7. How do you evaluate students?

Checklist of Lesson Plans

TEACHER'S NAME	SUBJECT	TOPICS	ON FILE

116

Textbook Survey Record Form

GRADE	SUBJECT	TITLE(S) OF TEXT(S)

Notes: (special features, authors included, general aids)

Textbook Survey Record Form

GRADE	SUBJECT	TITLE(S) OF TEXT(S)

Notes: (special features, authors included, general aids)

Cooperative Planning Guide

TOPIC

Yes ↓   No → | Consult course of study, curriculum guide, teacher |

CONTENT APPROACH?

Yes ↓   No → | Consult textbook, teacher's guide, teaching plan, teacher |

INSTRUCTIONAL TECHNIQUE?

Yes ↓   No → | Consult teaching plan, teacher |

TEACHING AIDS?

Yes ↓   No → | Consult AV list, preview material to match with teaching objectives |

ADDITIONAL INFORMATION SOURCES?

Yes ↓   No → | Consult core reference sources, identify relevant topics |

SUPPLEMENTARY MATERIALS?

Yes ↓   No → | Consult library catalog, reference lists in text, public library catalog, handbooks on topic |

LIBRARY MEDIA ACTIVITIES?

Yes ↓   No → | What, who, when, how long, evaluation method |

Model for Collaborative Planning

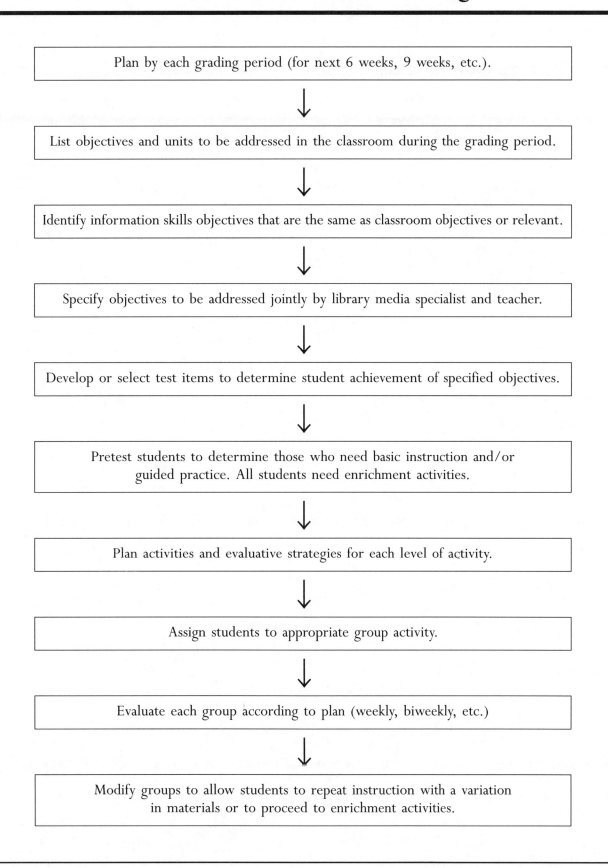

Plan by each grading period (for next 6 weeks, 9 weeks, etc.).

↓

List objectives and units to be addressed in the classroom during the grading period.

↓

Identify information skills objectives that are the same as classroom objectives or relevant.

↓

Specify objectives to be addressed jointly by library media specialist and teacher.

↓

Develop or select test items to determine student achievement of specified objectives.

↓

Pretest students to determine those who need basic instruction and/or guided practice. All students need enrichment activities.

↓

Plan activities and evaluative strategies for each level of activity.

↓

Assign students to appropriate group activity.

↓

Evaluate each group according to plan (weekly, biweekly, etc.)

↓

Modify groups to allow students to repeat instruction with a variation in materials or to proceed to enrichment activities.

Correlating Library Resources with the Curriculum

For each subject taught:

1. List the topics and skills to be addressed.

2. Review the table of contents and index of each textbook and make a note of the topics and skills that are addressed.

3. Identify and note the Dewey Decimal Classification for each topic.

4. Identify related titles in the collection and record the copyright date for each item. Note the number of items and judge the reading level of each.

5. Identify and note segments in general reference sources that address each topic.

6. Identify related information in periodicals, in the vertical file, and in the community resources file.

7. Identify related audiovisual information available in the school and system collections.

8. Identify fiction titles that relate to the topic.

Types of Information

Terminology

Pronunciation	☐	Opposite	☐
Part of speech	☐	Derivative	☐
Variation	☐	Abbreviation	☐
Meaning	☐	Acronym	☐
Root	☐	Slang	☐
Colloquialism	☐		

Statistics

Current ☐
Historical ☐
Representative ☐

Illustration

Analogy	☐	Model	☐
Symbol	☐	Example	☐
Picture	☐		

Fact

Name or label ☐
Statement ☐
Supporting facts ☐

Opinion

Quote	☐	Correspondence	☐
Editorial	☐	Position paper	☐

Place

Picture ☐
Location ☐
Definition ☐
Description: landscape, industry, culture ☐
    (language, dress, beliefs, practices, music, literature)

Process

Linear	☐	Systematic	☐

Materials

Audiovisual	☐	Illustration	☐
Poem	☐	Song	☐
Book	☐	Symbol	☐

Verbs Describing Learning Tasks

Knowing

Defining

Comparing

Identifying

Labeling

Listing

Locating

Matching

Selecting

Comprehending

Changing

Differentiating

Concluding

Illustrating

Interpreting

Predicting

Restating

Applying

Classifying

Demonstrating

Solving

Generalizing

Organizing

Producing

Analyzing

Categorizing

Deducing

Diagramming

Discriminating

Hypothesizing

Inferring

Interpreting

Synthesizing

Combining

Compiling

Constructing

Creating

Formulating

Originating

Revising

Evaluating

Assessing

Criticizing

Discriminating

Judging

Rating

Valuing

Sixth Grade Examples of Collaborative Planning

Language Arts   Explain the term "relevant." Provide examples of relevant information. Provide students with paragraphs drawn from appropriate textbooks and fiction books. Ask them to use a highlighter to indicate irrelevant details. Have students work in pairs so each student can check the other's work before class discussion.

Language Arts   Have students draw a picture of a classroom event, in which they have included several irrelevant details. Let other students identify the irrelevant details. Or provide students with poetry segments and ask them to write lines that would inject irrelevant details using rhymes.

Math   Prepare an activity board that shows the time in each zone when it is 5:00 p.m. in Greenwich, England. Give each student a sheet on which they must write in the time in each zone. Change the Greenwich time and have students make the appropriate adjustment on their activity sheets.

Math   Have students show the time zones using newsprint and the model found in *The World Almanac and Book of Facts*. Let students prepare labels with a variety of times indicated on each one. Have them test other students to see if they can place the labels correctly according to the time given for Greenwich.

Science   Providing appropriate encyclopedias and other texts, have students identify each bone in an illustration of the human skeleton.

Science   Invite a local emergency vehicle driver or orthopedic surgeon to talk with the class about frequent skeletal injuries, appropriate first aid, and treatment. Tickets to the session require labeling all specified bones on a skeleton handout.

Music   A video center features Latin and South American dancers. Students are expected to be able to recall details about dances, costumes, and musical instruments.

Art   Using selected slides from a National Gallery of Art series, students are asked to select one picture and to research either the artist, the content (such as clothing, food, or buildings), or the medium.

Eighth Grade Example of Contract Unit

American Revolution Unit

I. This will be a contract unit. You, the student, will decide what grade you are to receive.

   To receive an A — Five (5) activities and test
   To receive a B   — Four (4) activities and test
   To receive a C   — Three (3) activities and test

II. All students must do one activity from each group. If you contract for an A or B, your 4th and 5th activity may come from any of the three groups.

III. **Group I**

   1. Write a two-page essay or report on a historical figure of the American Revolution.
   2. Write a two-page book report on an approved book dealing with the American Revolution.
   3. Write a two-page editorial defending or condemning the rebellion of the British colonies.
   4. Write a two-page review of the movie.
   5. Compose a poem of at least one page which describes your feelings or thoughts on the American Revolution.

   Group II

   6. Draw a series of three political cartoons about the American Revolution.
   7. Construct a full color poster encouraging or discouraging participation in the American Revolution.
   8. Draw a full color picture of a figure from the American Revolution and write a one-page biography of that person.
   9. Construct a time line on a poster board which displays the major events leading up to and including the American Revolution.
   10. Complete a bulletin board dealing with the American Revolution.

   Group III

   11. Write, produce, and star in a one act play. Five to ten minutes dealing with any event, battle, or figure of the American Revolution (four people or less).
   12. Form two teams of students and debate the American Revolution from the American and English viewpoints (four people or less).
   13. Write and perform a rap dealing with the American Revolution or a historical figure from it.
   14. Give an oral report on a person or event of the American Revolution.
   15. Present a newscast of an important event of the American Revolution.

ALL ACTIVITIES ARE DUE ON _____ .

WRITTEN TEST WILL BE ON _____ .

Used with permission from Lisa Churchill, Library Media Specialist, Gresham Middle School, Birmingham, Alabama.

Information Skills Evaluation
Fifth Grade

Information skills objective: Use newspapers to obtain information on goods, services, and day-to-day events.

Content objectives: Specify the purpose of the daily newspaper guide.

Explain the purpose of the location symbol (page #).

Test items: How is a newspaper guide like a table of contents?

Explain how to find a certain section of the newspaper.

Performance task: Cut out guide from the number of newspapers equal to number of students in the group. Laminate guides. Attach one guide to a question sheet with questions similar to the following:

On what page will you find movies currently showing?

On what page will you find opinion statements of the newspaper editor?

On what page can you find a write-up of a ballgame?

On what page would you find an advertisement for used furniture?

On what page would you find a listing of television programs?

On what page would you find the most important news story of the day?

Information skills objective: Use a biographical dictionary to obtain information about a person.

Content objective: Know the purpose and organization of a biographical dictionary. Recognize that a policy is established by the publisher that governs which names will be included in any resource (this note is usually found in the preface).

Test items: Indicate the correct answer(s) by writing in the appropriate letter(s).

To find information about a famous person's life, you could look in   _____

    a. an encyclopedia   **d.** a newspaper
    b. a general dictionary   **e.** an almanac
    c. a biographical dictionary **f.** an atlas

A biographical dictionary is an alphabetized listing of information about   _____

    a. books   **c.** biographies
    b. people   **d.** biology

A biographical dictionary is arranged   _____
    a. chronologically   **c.** alphabetically
    b. in sections   **d.** numerically

Names included in a biographical dictionary were selected
according to   _____
    a. the compiler's choice   **c.** country in which the
    b. a certain characteristic   person lives or lived
        such as type of work   **d.** accomplishment

Performance task: Give each student a slip of paper with a different famous person's name. Have the student use a biographical dictionary, a general dictionary, and an encyclopedia to find information about the person. Have them compare length and content of each entry. Ask students to explain why a person's name is or is not included in one or more books.

Related materials: *Biography, Background for Inspiration,* Library Filmstrip Center

---

Information skills objective: Use a dictionary to locate homonyms (words pronounced alike but with different meanings), synonyms (words with the same meaning), and antonyms (words with opposite meanings).

Content objectives: Define each term and compare.

Identify synonyms and antonyms for a given word.

Write a sentence showing two uses of a given homonym.

Test items: Which word is a synonym for happy? _____
    a. gleeful   **b.** honey   **c.** charming   **d.** delicious

Which word is an antonym for happy? _____
    a. simple   **b.** sad   **c.** sorry   **d.** joppy

Which word is a homonym for Mary? _____
    a. name   **b.** Barry   **c.** merry   **d.** marry

Error means _____
    a. mistake   **b.** easy   **c.** truth   **d.** dull

Performance tasks: Given a specific word, develop a thesaurus (i.e., tan: beige, ecru, buff, sepia, honey, mocha).

Identify an antonym for each word in a given list.

Use the word "pool" in two different ways. (swimming pool, game of pool, car pool), rain/reign, bare/bear, hare/hair, blue/blew, stair/stare, sun/son, principle/principal, red/read, know/no

$\rightarrow$

Related materials: Terban, *Eight Ate: A Feast of Homonym Riddles*
Hanson, *Homonyms*
_____ , *More Homonyms*
_____ , *Still More Homonyms*

**Information
skills objective:**   Use alphabetical order to organize a bibliography.

Content objectives: Recognize bibliography as a list of resources.

Recognize a bibliography as a source of additional, similar information.

Recognize each source cited in a bibliography as an "entry."

Recognize alphabetical order as the usual arrangement of a bibliography.

Use alphabetical order to organize a bibliography.

Use alphabetical order to the third or fourth letter.

Test items:

1. Which title would be listed first in a bibliography, *Famous First Facts* or *Finding Information Fast*?

_____

2. Which author's work would be listed first in a bibliography, Bannon, Barber, Barron, or Baer?

_____

3. What is the purpose of a bibliography?

_____

4. How does a bibliography differ from a biography?

_____

Performance tasks: Locate a bibliography in a nonfiction book; in an encyclopedia.

Arrange the strips cut from a xeroxed bibliography into correct order.

Related materials: *Alphabetical Order* by Instructor (game board and spirit masters)

Information skills objective:	Recognize unrelated ideas.
Content objective:	Focus on a topic.
Test items:	1. Given three sentences, underline the one that is unrelated. Astronomy is the study of the universe. One of my favorite songs is "Stars Fell on Alabama." Astronomers have watched the sun, moon, and stars for hundreds of years.
	2. Which word is unrelated to the others? stars, sun, son, moon _____ simple, uncomplicated, easy, tight _____ toy, top, tomorrow, ball _____ work, labor, dig, yard _____
Performance task:	Identify a topic and write a paragraph in which all sentences are related.

Information skills objective:	Determine if sufficient information is provided to solve a problem.
Content objective:	Pose a question. Evaluate existing information to see if the question is answered.
Test items:	(Answer yes if you have enough information to answer the question.) Billy is going to town on his bicycle. He is supposed to meet his mother at 3:30 p.m. Will he be on time? _____ Thousands of years ago dinosaurs roamed this region. There are no more dinosaurs. Many theories exist about the conditions that led to the disappearance of dinosaurs from this region. Why did the dinosaurs disappear from this region? _____
Performance tasks:	1. Use a given nursery rhyme or folktale to determine what information is missing. • Jack & Jill went up a hill to fetch a pail of water. Jack fell down. • No one would help the Little Red Hen so she ate the food alone. 2. Photocopy a book passage and cut and paste it so a paragraph is missing. Ask the students to determine the missing information.
Related materials:	Lionni, *Pezzettino* Silverstein, *The Missing Piece* Silverstein, *The Missing Piece Meets the Big O*

**Information
skills objective:**   Compare and contrast information from a passage.

Content objectives: Identify the topic.

Identify supporting elements.

Separate supporting elements into similar and different categories.

Test items: Use literature passages or passages from nonfiction books.

Performance tasks: Given a short passage, categorize similar facts

"Mysterious monsters are monsters that may or may not exist. No one is absolutely sure. Fuzzy, unsatisfying photos have been snapped, footprints and bones have been found, and evidence that there really are such creatures turns up almost yearly. Still, no one has actually seen or touched them. So they remain mysterious and must be set apart in a category of their own." (from *Monster Magic,* Oryx Press, 1983).

Contrast:

Photos exist, footprints and bones have been found.

No one has seen or touched them.

**Information
skills objective:**   Recognize the use of propaganda.

Content objectives: Explain the meaning of the term, propaganda.

Identify techniques used to persuade, such as bandwagon, testimonials, slogans, and name-calling

Test items: Explain the purpose of propaganda.

What is it?

A company tries to convince you that you will be more popular if you wear the tennis shoe they make.

A famous movie star says she prefers Brand X.

"We're not the biggest, just the best."

Dr. Pepper hits the spot!

Performance tasks: Highlight the words in an ad that attempt to persuade.

Select ads from a newspaper or magazine and explain if and/or how the ad uses propaganda.

→

**Information
skills objective:**   Identify the author's purpose.

Content objectives: Identify an author as the originator of a piece of material.

Recognize purposes for writing: inform, inquire, convince, entertain.

Test items: Identify the author's purpose for each segment (draw from literature).

"Mrs. Mantis catches bugs,

Squashes them with mighty hugs,"   _____

"Then I saw a bullfight. It's a sport where the bullfighter fools the bull with

a cloth cape and kills it with a sword."   _____

"For good health, it is important to eat food from each of the four food

groups every day and to drink eight glasses of water."   _____

"We are looking for a dog with black curly hair and long floppy ears. Have

you seen a dog that looks like this?"   _____

Performance tasks: Distribute strips of paper upon which are written one of the purposes for writing. Ask students to find in books or write examples illustrating that purpose. Have student pairs or teams compete.

Let student draw slip from box. Each slip has a different purpose for writing. The student must compose an appropriate piece. To make this task more difficult, have two boxes. Box 1 directs the student toward the type of writing and Box 2 dictates the topic.

**Information
skills objective:**   Distinguish among myths, legends, and fables.

Content objectives: Recognize a myth as a story that explains why people have a certain belief or practice, or explain a natural phenomenon.

Recognize a legend as a story that reveals past history, although history that is not usually verifiable.

Recognize a fable as a story about supernatural happenings.

Test items:	Stories about Paul Bunyan are:
	a. myths **b.** fables **c.** legends _____
	Stories about a Roman god causing thunder and lightning are:
	a. myths **b.** fables **c.** legends _____
	Stories about a man swallowed by a whale are: _____
Performance tasks:	Make up a fable, myth, or legend.
	Make a list of story characters by category (myth, legend, and fable).
	Compare and contrast characters from myths, legends, and fables.

**Information
skills objective:** Read and interpret line and bar graphs.

Content objectives: Recognize that charts and graphs are representative.

Recognize that the intersection of two factors is needed for a line or bar graph to be meaningful.

Ability to pinpoint the intersection of two factors.

Test items: Given a line or bar graph on paper or transparency, answer the following questions: (Examples depend upon graph.)

What cities have the largest population?

What day had the highest temperature?

Note: Almanacs and *U.S.A. Today* are good sources

Performance task: Make a bar chart or line graph to represent the height of each person in your group.

Related materials: *Graph and Practice Skills Kit,* Science Research Associates (programmed text)

Key Words to Use in Evaluation

Response

select, match, distinguish, check, circle, connect, label, list, classify, subdivide, outline, design

Record, oral or written

give examples, name, comment, express, compare, criticize, correct, report, revise

Manipulatives

name, select, match, connect, label, organize, calculate, make, classify

Perform

illustrate, discover, locate, point out, memorize, role play

Product

mural, diorama, transparency, chart, graph, picture, outline, time line, model, videotape, audiotape, database

Question, oral or written

recall, complete, describe, explain, report, translate

Discussion, oral or written

compare, contrast, summarize, estimate, relate, generalize, conclude

Illustrate

draw, role play, dramatize

Record-Keeping Forms

Materials in this appendix are for library media specialists to use or adapt in implementing a curriculum-based program.

Teacher Survey Form

A form to use when getting to know each faculty member.

Teacher Planning Chart

A form, arranged by teacher's name and room number, to keep a record of whether or not the monthly planning session has been held.

Library Assignment Pass

Filled out as the teacher plans for the day's events, this form serves as a hall pass and reminds the student and library media specialist about the expected product. Passes with each teacher's name and grade level should be prepared in advance.

Performance Chart 1

A form providing the library media specialist with a checklist for information skill development by students. Requires that each skill be successfully demonstrated before a check is placed under the student's name.

Performance Chart 2

A form providing the library media specialist with a checklist for students learning to use specific reference sources.

Student Record Card

This form can be completed by the student as self-evaluation or by the teacher or library media specialist. The activity to be accomplished should be identified clearly and criteria for success be understood.

Student Assignment Card

A second form that can be used for self-evaluation. Provides a good starting point for a teacher or library media specialist and student discussion about the library assignment.

Library Media Student Assignment

A form for a teacher and the library media specialist to use when assigning students to particular groups. This form is set up for six students to a group but not all spaces have to be filled if a smaller group is desired. This form allows the professionals to have an overview of group assignments to prevent students consistently being placed in similar groups.

Teacher Survey Form

Name: _____   Date completed: _____

Subject(s) taught: _____

_____

_____

Favorite topics: _____   _____

_____   _____

Preferred teaching strategy:

_____

Preferred grouping strategy:

_____

Experiences with media:

_____

_____

Best planning time: Day _____   Period _____

Professional development goals:

_____

_____

Teacher Planning Chart

Name	Room	Sept.	Oct.	Nov.	Dec.	Jan.	Feb.	Mar.	Apr.	May

LIBRARY ASSIGNMENT PASS

Teacher _____

Grade _____   Number of students _____

Subject _____

Assigned task _____

_____

Expected product _____

Return to class by _____

LIBRARY ASSIGNMENT PASS

Teacher _____

Grade _____   Number of students _____

Subject _____

Assigned task _____

_____

Expected product _____

Return to class by _____

Acquisition of Information Skills

Information Skill	Student Names				

Note: Fill in the skill to be learned; e.g., arrange ideas in sequential order.

Use of Reference Sources

Student Names:						
Thesaurus						
Poetry Index						
Propaganda						
Abbreviations						
Symbols						
Catalog Entries						
Tables & Graphs						
Newspaper Sections						
Citations						
Newsmakers						
Antonyms						
Almanac						
Atlas						

Student Record Card

Name: _____   **Class:** _____

Date(s)	Activity	Rating (Circle)
		Successful Partly successful Unsuccessful

Student Record Card

Name: _____   **Class:** _____

Date(s)	Activity	Rating (Circle)
		Successful Partly successful Unsuccessful

Student Assignment Card

Name: _____ Date: _____

Topic: _____

Objective: _____

Assignment: _____

_____

Probable information source: _____

1. How did I do? (Circle one)

     Ooops!   2   3   4   Fantastic!

2. What did I learn?

_____

_____

_____

3. What did I learn about myself?

_____

_____

_____

_____

Library Media Student Assignment

Activity: _____

Unit			
Unit			
Unit			
Unit			
Unit			

Index

Administering the School Library Media Center, 91
Administration, survey. *See* Faculty, survey
Alexander, William, 14
American Association of School Librarians, 44
American Libraries, 83
American Newspaper Publishers Association
    Foundation, 81
"Art Access" exhibits, 83
Art in the Basic Curriculum ("ABC"), 83
Assessment vs. evaluation, 89–91

Bibliographies for counselors, 77
Bibliotherapy, 76
Block schedules. *See* Schedules, flexible
Body changes. *See* Preadolescents, development
Book discussion groups, 77, 78
Bridging the Gap: What's Happening Now, 84
Buchanan, Jan, 54

Canadian Daily Newspaper Publishers Association, 81
Career and college information, 79
Center for Early Adolescence, 23
Certification requirements, 50
Checklists. *See* Forms
Cleaver, Betty, 55
Collection correlation, 36–37
Coming of Age, 84
"Communicate through Literature," 86
Community involvement and media services, 84–88
Community Resource File, 85
Community Services File, 85
Community survey, 26–28
Community Volunteer File, 85
Consulting, instructional, 41, 42
Continuous progress program, 15, 18
Contribution to School Goals form, 91, 92

Contributions to the Instructional Program form, 91,
    93
Cooperative Planning Guide, 55, 118
Correlating Library Resources with the Curriculum
    form, 120
Counseling. *See* Guidance programs and media services
Course objectives. *See* Objectives, instructional
Curriculum-based program. *See* Library media
    program
Curriculum committee, 32. *See also* Library media
    committee
Curriculum guide, 32
Curriculum map, 46–47
Curzon, Susan, 6

Displays, of student work, 78

Eichhorn, Donald, 14
Emergency Librarian, 83
Equipment operation skills, 62, 63–66
ERIC, 81
Evaluation, 132
    definition, 89–90
    forms, 90, 91
    information skills, 125–31
    of library media activities, 52–54, 57
    of library media program, 89–104
Exploratory courses, 75, 84
Exploratory programs and media services, 80–84

Faculty survey, 27, 30–31
Farley Elementary School, 6
Files
    community resource, 75, 85
    community services, 75, 85
    community volunteer, 85

Flexible Access Library Media Programs, 54
Forms
    community involvement, 85
    evaluation, 90–104
    instructional planning, 54–57, 113–32
    library media program planning, 105–12
    record-keeping, 133–42
Foxfire, 82
Fullan, Michael, 1

Georgia Department of Education, 6
Gifted students, 79
Goodlad, John, 8
Government agency resources, 81–82
Greenville (S.C.) Middle School, 86
Group discussions, 75
Guidance programs and media services, 75, 76–80
Guidelines, library media program, 44
Gustafson, Kent, 52, 91

Handicapped students, 79
Harper's Choice Middle School, 14, 21, 86–87
Hatcher, Robert, 84
Haycock, Carol-Ann, 3
High Museum of Art, Atlanta, 83
Home base provision, 20
Home environment survey, 29
Hug, Bill, 48

Information objectives. *See* Objectives, information
    skills
*Information Power: Guidelines for School Library Media
    Programs,* 32, 41
Information Skill Instruction form, 100
Information skills, teaching, 61–72
    defined, 61
    evaluation, 125–31
    record-keeping, 62
    relating to course content, 67
    remediation, 70
    sample objectives, 62, 63–67
    student knowledge, testing, 67
Information types, 70, 121
Instruction, individualized, 16, 18–19
Instructional activities. *See* Library media activities
*The Instructional Consultant Role of the School Library
    Media Specialist,* 55
Instructional consulting, 41, 42
Instructional Design and the Media Program, 48
Instructional design process, 48–50, 60
Instructional Intent of Teachers form, 115

Instructional objectives. *See* Objectives, instructional
Instructional planning aids and examples, 113–32
Instructional program survey, 32–37
Instructional Technology, 52
Intramural activities, 22

Knirk, Fred, 52

Learning tasks, describing, 122
Lesson plans, 34, 46, 50, 116
Library Assignment Pass, 137
Library media activities, 43, 46–60. *See also* Library
    media services
    curriculum map, 46–47
    evaluation, 52–54, 57
    group discussions, 75, 77
    and parents, 87
    planning. *See* Planning
    scheduling, 59–60
    selection of materials for, 51
    variation of, 53
Library media center
    as an arts center, 78, 86
    instructional support service, 111
    instructional validity and, 57
    newsletter, 87
    philosophy, 107
    as a place to be alone, 19–20
    as a place to interact, 20, 78
Library Media Center Pass, 57
Library media committee, 43–44, 105, 108–9
Library media program, 1–12. *See also* Middle school
    program
    centralized position within the school, 47
    change from traditional to curriculum-based, 1–8
    classroom information, enhancing, 70
    collection correlation with the curriculum, 120
    curriculum-based, 2–4, 8–10
    effective, 44
    evaluation of, *see* Evaluation, library media
        program
    goal and objectives, 2, 3, 7, 96–99
    guidelines, 44
    and individual needs, 7, 76–78
    instructional program survey, 32–37
    materials. *See* Materials
    planning, 39–45
    priorities, 41–42, 44
    scheduling, 4, 6, 10, 20–22
    and school goals, 30
    school survey. *See* School survey
    videotaped examples, 6

Library media services, 41–42, 44. *See also* Library media activities
    exploratory programs and, 80–84
    guidance programs and, 75, 76–80
    Instructional Support Services form, 111
    isolation from the school program, 41
    priorities of, 42, 44
Library media specialist
    certification requirements for, 50
    as a change agent, 4, 6, 7
    classroom instruction, supporting, 49–50, 53, 60
    as a communications agent for the school, 87
    as an educator, 8
    exploratory courses, teaching, 84
    as an instructional consultant, 2, 47, 53
    and the instructional design process, 4, 48
    management role of, 58
    as a member of the curriculum committee, 32
    as a member of the school team, 6, 8, 10, 30, 48
    and parents, 86
    planning, involvement in, 7, 17
    relationship with other faculty, 3, 5–6, 8, 10, 30, 47, 76, 79–80
    school environment, understanding, 13, 26
    self-development process, contribution to, 13, 73–74
    as a special librarian, 26
Library Media Student Assignment form, 142
Library media use indicators, 105, 110
Library skills. *See* Information skills
Lipsitz, Joan, 23
Location and retrieval skills, 62, 63–66
Loertscher, David, 3

Master schedule of instruction, 47
Materials
    developed locally, 51–52
    for exploratory programs, 80–84
    for guidance programs, 76–77
    selecting, 51–53
    supplementary, reviewing, 37
    variety, 18
Media committee. *See* Library media committee
Media services. *See* Library media services
Media skills. *See* Information skills
Middle school program, 14–25. *See also* Library media program
    characteristics of, 14–16
    materials, *see* Materials
    scheduling, 20–22
    and student characteristics, 16, 22–24

Model for Collaborative Planning, 118
Monthly Catalog, 81
Morris, Betty, 91
Multi-use areas, 19
Museums and galleries as resources, 83

National Association of Secondary School Principals, 84
Newsletter, library media center, 87
Newspaper in Education Program, 81
Newspapers in instruction, 80–81

Objectives
    information skills, 55, 62, 63–67
    instructional, 55, 67–70
    involving, 86, 87
    of library media program, 7
    survey, 27, 29

Peer interaction, 15, 19, 23
Performance Chart forms, 71, 138–39
Personalized instruction. *See* Instruction, individualized
Physical education, 22
Planning
    collaborative, 119, 123–24
    cooperative, forms for, 55, 118
    cooperative, need for, 3–4, 17
    forms, 54–57, 105–12, 113–32
    frequency of, 59
    instructional, aids and examples, 113–32
    library media activities, 46–60
    library media program, 39–45
    model, 39–41
    priorities, 41–42
    record, 58–59
Pod arrangement, 19
Policies and procedures, survey, 31
Preadolescents. *See also* Students
    adults, need for contact with, 23, 24
    concerns of, 77
    development, 14, 15, 22–24, 73–75, 84
    educating, 14
    group association, 15, 19–20, 23, 75
    independence, need to assert, 74
    insecurity in, 19, 22, 74
    instructional needs of, 16–19
    preoccupation with self, 74
    socialization, 78
Presentation skills, 62, 63–66
Principals, persuading to change, 7

Principal's Questionnaire, 102–4
Production services, 41
Production skills, 62, 63–66
Professional Improvement and Practices Checklist,
    91, 101
Professional resources, 83–84
Program planning committee. *See* Library media
    committee

Questionnaires. *See* Forms
"Quiet corners," providing, 19–20

Recorder, library media committee, 44
Record-keeping forms, 133–42
Record-keeping, information skills, 62
Regional resources, 82–83
Reminders for Today form, 106, 112
Research for School Library Media Specialists, 91
Research skills, 62, 63–66
Resources in Education, 81–82
Response to Library Media Program Goals and
    Objectives form, 96–99
Riggs, Virginia, 81
Role models, 20, 24
Rules and penalties, 24

Saint Louis (Mo.) Art Museum, 83
Scales, Pat, 86
Schedules, flexible, 4, 10, 20–22
    videotapes describing, 6
Scheduling, library media activities, 59–60
School Library Journal, 83
School Library Media Quarterly, 83
School media specialist. *See* Library media specialist
School survey, 26–38
    checklist, 27
    collection analysis, 36–37
    community, 26–28
    facility, 27, 28
    faculty, 27, 30–31
    goals, 31
    history, 27, 28–29
    instructional program, 32–37
    lesson plans, 34, 46, 116
    objectives, 32
    parents, 27, 29
    policies and procedures, 31

supplementary materials, 37
    test results, 34
    textbooks, 34–36
Seeley, Pris, 6
Smith, Jane, 91
Stanek, Lou, 83
State and regional resources, 82–83
Student(s). *See also* Middle school program;
    Preadolescents
    gifted, 79
    government, 24
    grouping, 10, 19–20
    handicapped, 79
    home environment, 29
    involvement in learning, 17
    needs, understanding, 13–25
Student Assignment Card, 141
Student Record Card, 70, 140
Study Guide for a Mini-Course on Death, 83
Study skills, improving, 78
"Suitcase Exhibits," 83
Surveys. *See* School survey

Taylor, William, 55
Teacher Alert, 106, 111
Teacher Planning Chart, 136
Teacher Survey form, 135
Teachers
    and change, 7, 8
    instructional intent, questionnaire, 115
Teaching objectives. *See* Objectives, instructional
Technical review of titles, 34–36
Test data, reviewing, 46
Test results, survey, 34
Textbook Survey Record form, 117
Textbooks, reviewing, 34–36, 46
Thinking skills, 62, 63–66
Time Accountability form, 91, 94
Time Summary Sheet, 91, 95
Transescents, 14. *See also* Preadolescents

Videotapes of curriculum-based programs, 6
Volunteer program, 85

Wigginton, Eliot, 82
Wilkerson Middle School, 105